The Cruelest Death

The Cruelest Death

The Enigma of Adolescent Suicide

David Lester, PhD

The Charles Press, Publishers
Philadelphia

The Charles Press, Publishers
Post Office Box 15715
Philadelphia, PA 19103

Library of Congress Cataloging-in-Publication Data

Lester, David, 1942-
      The cruelest death: the enigma of adolescent suicide / David Lester.
      p.   cm.
   Includes bibliographical references.
   ISBN 0-914783-64-5
   1. Teenagers — Suicidal behavior.   2. Teenagers — United States — Suicidal behavior.   I. Title.
   HV6546.L47 1992
   362.2'8'0835 — dc20   92-34448
                                                                   CIP

ISBN 0-914783-64-5

Printed in the United States of America

Contents

Introduction

The incidence of adolescent suicide has increased dramatically during the past 20 years. In fact, suicide is now the third leading cause of death in the United States among persons under the age of 24. It is estimated that no less than 300,000 young people will attempt to kill themselves this year. More than 6000 will succeed.

What has caused this suicide epidemic? Why do so many young people want to end their lives? Certainly, it can be argued that, on the whole, young people today have more material wealth than any other generation, but apparently, this does not necessarily mean that they are happier. Indeed, many attribute suicide among adolescents to the complexities of today's world. For many reasons times are more difficult and stressful than before, especially for today's youth, and the increasing suicide rate is an index of this pain.

There are various factors that may contribute to this problem. Lack of a solid family unit, lack of clear-cut goals, lack of self-esteem, lack of (or bad) role models, and a breakdown of communication between peers and parents are just a few of the burdens with which today's youth may be faced. Add to this the increase in domestic violence, the ever-increasing divorce rate and the destruction of the family unit and it is not hard to understand why life today may be exceedingly hard for young people to handle.

A difficulty we face in trying to understand how to intervene is that many young people suffer from some or all of the limitations above, but few of them choose suicide as their way out. Young people with very similar problems may react with completely different responses; one may commit suicide, another may commit a crime, and still another may find the strength to solve the problem. What are the reasons for these differences in behavior and how can we predict who will commit suicide?

Few reasons have been determined thus far, and it is fair to say that adolescent suicide is an enigma to most of us. We do not understand how a young person, with his whole life ahead of him, would despair of hope and choose to kill himself. This behavior in adults is somewhat more understandable. If we can't explain or accurately predict adolescent suicide, where does this leave the clinician and parent, and how can they help prevent suicide?

First and foremost, the clinician must appreciate the many differences between adult and adolescent thinking and he must not judge an adolescent's response to situations from an adult standpoint. For one thing, depression, a key factor in both adult and adolescent suicide, may present itself in entirely different ways in these two groups: an adult may respond with lethargy and lack of motivation, while a youngster may respond with aggression.

Unlike other books on this subject, which leave the impression that awareness, discussion and a diligent approach will inevitably be successful, I have resisted the idea that prevention is just a matter of following a prescribed method: reason with a kid and he will surely see your point.

Because adolescents tend to choose suicide for different reasons than adults, and because they often view matters in ways that are markedly different from their elders, any study that simply glides over the differences will fall short of its objectives. Once suicide prevention strategies are successfully linked to those studies that see adolescent behavior as an age-specific phenomenon, crisis workers, parents and society will have a real, reasonable chance to reverse a most tragic trend.

The Cruelest Death

Chapter 1

Two Cases of Youth Suicide

Before beginning a more formal discussion of suicide in adolescents and young adults, it would be useful to present two detailed case histories of suicide in young people. The information about each case has been taken from books that were written by the respective parents of two young men who committed suicide. We have chosen the suicide of an adolescent who did not appear to have any sort of serious emotional problems and the suicide of a young man who was very obviously psychiatrically disturbed in order to illustrate the different life styles we find in young suicides and the different problems they present.

JODY WHITE

Jody White shot himself at the age of 17. After he died his mother, Susan, wrote a book about Jody's life and death (White-Bowden 1985). Starting with the history of their family, Susan informed us that she had gotten married secretly when she was 15 to John White, 8 years her senior. They had two children,

1

both girls, and then Susan became pregnant again. John did not want a third child and urged Susan to have an abortion, a procedure that at the time was not legal. She refused and had Jody on March 8, 1960. Their daughter Majorie was 4 and daughter O'Donnell was 17 months old when Jody was born.

The family lived in a house that they had built on Susan's family farm. Their marriage was in trouble from the start. In fact, during their honeymoon Susan realized that she had made a mistake in her decision to marry John. They disagreed about everything, and John was very domineering. Susan described their sex life as good but felt that there was a lack of open and honest communication between them. After John had several affairs, the two separated twice before finally getting divorced.

Early Years

Susan described her son Jody as a placid, easy and happy child. He did, however, have a speech impediment. His father's method of "helping" him was to punish harshly, often preventing the boy from eating, for example, until he correctly pronounced the words. After Jody was ridiculed at school, his mother took him to a speech therapist who helped correct the problem.

Susan and her daughters spoiled Jody except on the rare occasions when John was home. John wanted his son to be strong, unemotional and mature. He forbade everyone in the family to hug and kiss Jody and even punished the boy for giggling and crying.

However, when Jody was 8, he and his father began to develop a closer relationship. When Jody wanted a minibike, his father told him to save his allowance and then helped him buy one. They rode and worked on their bikes together. Soon Jody was competing in and winning bike races. Despite their improved relationship, his father was still overly punitive, actually screaming at Jody when he lost a race.

After the Divorce

After 4 years of separations and reconciliations Jody's parents ended up getting a divorce when he was 14. He and his two sisters lived with their mother, who at the time worked as a reporter for a local television station. Her job took up a good deal of time; her hours were long and she did not go home to her children until after the early evening news. Near the time of the divorce she fell in love with a fellow reporter named Jack Bowden.

Jody's father refused to accept the finality of the divorce. He often came over to his family's house and would beg for another reconciliation. One day in November, 1974, John tried once more to persuade Susan to let him return, telling her that he could not live without her. As always, Susan refused. That night after dinner, while Susan was taking a bath, John shot himself in her bedroom with a handgun.

In retrospect, Susan felt that after the suicide of their father she didn't share her feelings with her children or allow them to talk about theirs. She didn't think of getting counseling for the family. (O'Donnell and Majorie went for counseling later in their lives.) While Susan does not explain how Jody reacted to his father's death, she does say that Jody did not cry at the funeral. They coped as best they could and tried to get on with life. Jody and O'Donnell went back to school, and Majorie took a year off before going to college. Jody continued to race his bikes. His mother took up bike riding and accompanied him to the race meetings on weekends. To Susan, Jody did not seem depressed at all.

Jody was successful at racing his bike, had a nice group of friends and some women who admired him. He was shy though, and hated talking on the telephone. This shyness seemed to worsen as he entered adolescence.

About three months after Jody's father's suicide, Susan had to go to a party and, since O'Donnell was also going out, Jody had to stay home by himself. This upset him and when his mother called him from the party, he hung up on her. Susan rushed home to see what was wrong; she somehow expected him to have killed himself and was relieved to find him alive. She felt guilty over abandoning him that night and promised never to do it again. She also mentioned that she felt guilty that she had developed the habit of buying Jody whatever he wanted, such as bicycles, whereas his father would have made him earn them.

When he turned 15, Jody moved up to the next class in bike racing and as a result did not win as often as he did in the past. Regardless of this he seemed quite happy that year; at least this is what his mother thought. He and his mother seemed close and they would often ride bikes together just for fun. Jody's sister Majorie went off to college in New England and, on the whole, the family seemed to be coping well. Jack Bowden, Susan's boyfriend, visited frequently, often bringing with him his 6-year-old son, Christopher, from his former marriage.

Jody met his first girlfriend that year, a 13-year-old who also rode bikes. When he was 16, Jody fell in love with another girl, Lauren, who at first chased Jody, but then, once they got together, rebelled against his possessiveness and caused him a lot of anguish. When she would refuse to go out with him, Jody would sometimes wait outside her house to see if she went out with someone else, in the same way his father had when dating his mother.

At the end of the school year, Jody destroyed several library book cards and unscrewed some fixtures at the private school he attended. Because he at first denied doing this, he broke the honor code and the school expelled him. However, Jody told his mother that he hated the school and so he quit before receiving the notice of expulsion. He enrolled in a polytechnic institute for his final two years of high school.

That summer, Susan White and Jack Bowden decided to get engaged, though their concerns about whether it was the wisest decision caused them to postpone the actual marriage. However, they did sleep together at this point when the children were at home. When his mother told Jody about her engagement, his response was, "I don't care." Susan says she wondered whether Jody was jealous of the attention that she gave to Jack's son Christopher.

The polytechnic school had thousands of students compared to the hundreds he was used to at his private school, but Jody seemed to do well. In February, 1977, Jody crashed his sister's car while high on marijuana. When his mother confronted him, Jody told her he had only been smoking it for a short time and claimed that he needed it to feel better and to study. Susan asked him at least not to drive while he was high and to try to cut down on his use. Jody agreed. (In retrospect, Susan said she wished that she had forbidden him to use pot altogether and that she wished that she had sought counseling of some kind for him.)

Since his mother didn't get home until 8:15 every night, Jody would come home to an empty house at 4:00, (his sisters were both away at college), go to a friend's house to do his homework and then go home again after 8:00 when his mother would fix dinner.

Gradually, Jody's relationship with Lauren began to cause him more and more pain. Jody competed in a bike race that month and rode well, coming in second in the first race. Because he had not raced since Christmas, when he broke his arm after crashing into a friend's bike, he was weak and crashed repeatedly in the second race. He seemed depressed with his performance and it turned out to be the last time he raced. He probably felt worse because Lauren had been there to witness his poor performance. Susan tried to get him to work on a fitness program to get his strength back, but he seemed uninterested.

On May 9, 1977, while she was getting ready for the evening news program, Susan got a telephone call from her daughter who was at home. Jody had shot and killed himself with a rifle in his bedroom. He left a suicide note saying that he had done so because of Lauren and later conversations with Lauren revealed that he had indeed threatened to kill himself if she didn't go back with him. Just before he killed himself he had called Lauren to tell her he was going to shoot himself and to say goodbye. (He had told some other friends a month earlier that he was going to kill himself because Lauren didn't love him and that his father had not loved him either.) Susan White found the book *The Little Prince* on the desk in his room, a story in which the hero commits suicide and whose author committed suicide soon after writing it.

Discussion

Jody's suicide seems remarkably like his father's. Both shot themselves in their bedrooms because of rejection from the women they loved. Both killed themselves in such a way as to maximize the guilt felt by their loved ones. Jody's mother notes the similarity between her son's reaction to Lauren's rejection and her husband's similar behavior when he tried to get her to remarry him.

Jody certainly did not work through the feelings of grief he had after his father's suicide. His mother noted that she was not used to communicating feelings and that she preferred to pretend things were fine. She called herself a "Susie Sunshine." She admitted that she ought to have obtained grief counseling for the family and drug counseling for Jody. She said that she ought to have spent more time with Jody and communicated her love for him.

As mentioned, Jody eventually became close to his father although this was not the case at first. The similarities between his behavior and his father's show that Jody identified strongly with him. This can be seen in the way he modelled his suicide so closely on his father's. In fact, his father seems to be the critical influence in Jody's life. (It is noteworthy that, so far as we know, Jody's two sisters have never been suicidal.)

Jody does not appear to have been psychiatrically disturbed and his drug use does not appear to have been extensive; as far as we know, he used only marijuana and his problems with girlfriends are quite typical of teenagers. His expulsion from school seems at best to have served his goals. Although his father was dead, Jody continued to identify with him; this may have led to an internal need to excel. For example, failing to win the bike race may have been excessively stressful for him. His relationship with Lauren seems to have been the critical precipitating factor in his suicide. The stress that he was experiencing with her may have been exacerbated by his poor performance in the bike race and his inability to cope with failure.

In conclusion, the striking feature of Jody's suicide is its imitative aspect. What makes it interesting is that the imitation followed so soon after his father's suicide.

MICHAEL WECHSLER

Michael Wechsler killed himself after a long period of psychiatric illness at the age of 26. His story was written and published in 1972 by his father, James Wechsler, a well-known journalist, but the biography seems far from objective because it is colored by the grief, anger and puzzlement felt by the father.

Early Life

In his book, Mr. Wechsler quickly skips over Michael's first 17 years and his account gives us no clues as to the genesis of Michael's disorder. Judging from what his father wrote, Michael was a happy and healthy boy until his breakdown. Michael did not agree; he stated that he did have problems and blamed them on his parents.

Michael was born in 1942, the Wechsler's first child. He seemed fine as baby, although he was perhaps a little precocious. His sister, Holly, was born four years later. Michael objected to her crib being in his room, and so Holly slept with her parents. When Michael was four, he fussed about going to sleep and when he finally did, he often walked in his sleep.

He was active, sociable, friendly and mature. When he was seven, his mother, who was a lawyer, became ill with mononucleosis. Michael helped out by making breakfast for the family in the morning. He had firm ideas about what he wanted, and he showed great persistence. He usually had a hobby that absorbed him — painting, the piano, chemistry, radio sets, photography, music, and model rockets. However, he did not date much in high school.

Interestingly, his sister had more adjustment problems than Michael; she went into therapy with a psychiatrist who was a long-time friend of the family, and this caused her to miss a good deal of school. Wechsler does not tell us what sort of problems Holly had.

Michael was sent to a private school (The Fieldston School) in fourth grade and by high school his work was excellent, though as he got older he and his friends withdrew from the social mainstream of his class. He was admitted to Harvard University in 1960.

In retrospect, the only signs of trouble in Michael were a tendency to want to be nothing less than perfect at everything he did and the fact that he deliberately created a distance from his father. Michael did not seem interested in journalism and sports like his father was, and Mr. Wechsler states that Michael's interests were more similar to his grandfather's than his father's. Mr. Wechsler often commented that he frequently did not know what to say to his son or how to relate to him. Conversations were muted and limited, but they were not hostile. Mr. Wechsler notes that their home life was hectic and turbulent; there were both public tensions — Wechsler was called before the McCarthy investigating committee when Michael was eleven — and conflicts in the parents' marriage.

The Beginning of Trouble

In the spring of his senior year of high school, Michael called his father and asked him to pay for him to see a psychiatrist. Michael had already located one, and his father agreed. Mr. Wechsler says that this request came out of the blue and that he had no warning of any impending problems. He does note, however, that he was so consumed by his career as a journalist that he had little time for his family; his lack of awareness of any problems does not mean that there were no warning signs.

From the start, Wechsler was hostile and argumentative

with Michael's psychiatrist and this became a pattern with all future psychiatrists. He called the first psychiatrist to request a meeting with him, but the psychiatrist refused. Wechsler was shocked by this and by other decisions made by the many other psychiatrists who treated Michael over the years. It may be that Wechsler had virtually no previous contact with the psycho-therapeutic profession and was therefore unaware of the rules and code of ethics that govern it. (Some therapists refuse to meet with the parents of a client because it undermines the trust that the client should have for the therapist. Meeting with the parents of a client might raise the question of whose side the therapist is on.) It might also be, however, that Wechsler's demand to be included in his son's therapy was characteristic of his style as a father; he was absent for much of the time and perhaps this was an attempt to make up for that. If the latter is true, it might account for Michael's hostility toward his father for it would be easier to accept intrusion from a father who was close to his children and had a less imperious style.

This first psychiatrist eventually consented to see Mr. and Mrs. Wechsler and told them that Michael's problem might require many years of treatment and that he may possibly need treatment for the rest of his life. The psychiatrist said Michael had obsessive thoughts, particularly about feces.

Michael saw the psychiatrist regularly until he went away to school at Harvard. He was generally anxious and uncommunicative during that time. The psychiatrist thought that Michael could survive at Harvard without treatment and that it was sufficient for Michael and him to have meetings only during holiday trips to New York.

At Harvard, Michael was much more withdrawn and lonely than he had been when he was in high school. He drove home most weekends. By Christmas, Michael seemed anxious about not seeing his psychiatrist more often. It was decided that Michael should see a therapist in Cambridge, and a family friend located one for him. However, Michael and the new therapist did not get along well, and the contact soon ended. His New York psychiatrist found him a therapist in Cambridge who Michael saw during his sophomore year. Michael and he got on better, but Michael's father was unhappy because this new therapist wanted little to do with the parents.

Before returning to Harvard for his sophomore year, Michael's therapist persuaded his parents to buy him a car. They did so reluctantly since he had had an accident in their car two years earlier. While driving home from Harvard on a Friday evening several months later, Michael fell asleep at the wheel and crashed. After his sophomore year, Michael stayed in Cambridge to work in the psychology laboratory and persuaded his parents to buy him a motorbike. In October Michael was seriously injured in a crash with a bus, an accident for which the bus driver admitted responsibility. Michael remained in the hospital for over three months and returned to Harvard in February 1963 on crutches.

To catch up on the missed semester, Michael decided to attend summer school. His junior year seemed better. His therapist in Cambridge decided to end regular visits because he thought that Michael had improved. Michael mentioned having friends at the university and seemed more at home there than he had in the past. Then out of the blue, Michael informed his parents that he had flunked one examination in the spring semester of 1964 and that he had obtained permission to waive two other exams. At this time he began to see his therapist again.

At the therapist's insistence, Michael's mother went to Cambridge to meet the therapist, who told her that her son had attempted suicide with an overdose of tranquilizers and that he had to go to the university infirmary to have his stomach pumped. The therapist also revealed that Michael had used drugs, and he suggested that the boy take a year off from college.

During this period Michael was tense all the time and often angry at his father. Following a session at the end of June, his therapist decided to hospitalize Michael for a couple of months. Michael was miserable as an inpatient and made several suicidal gestures, such as putting his hand through a window in his room and trying to hang himself. Eventually he left without permission and, after staying with friends for a few days, went home to his parents.

Hospitals and Death

Although Michael wanted to return to Harvard, it became clear that he was too distressed to do so. He looked for an apartment and a job, but failed to find either. He stayed home and shunned all of his friends. A therapist was found for him, his fourth, this time a woman. Michael's father persuaded a friend who ran a store to find him a job. Michael had no confidence in his ability to perform well but agreed to start working as a credit clerk. He began to visit his friends, one of whom found him an apartment.

At this time, Michael became preoccupied with playing his flute. He also began to take drugs, including LSD. Although he did well at work initially, getting a raise and the offer of a promotion, he eventually became unreliable and erratic in his work habits and because of this he was fired. After working for a month in a car rental agency, Michael decided to quit work to devote himself to the flute. He had occasional grandiose schemes, such as building a harpsichord and starting a coffee house, but these came to nought.

In late May 1965, Michael was picked up by the police while high on LSD. His parents found a psychiatrist who placed him in an expensive private psychiatric hospital. From there Michael was persuaded to go to a state hospital that had a reputation for having a good program, and he remained there from July 1965 to August 1966, although during that time he ran away eight times. His depression increased, and his failure both to improve his life and to return to Harvard weighed heavily on him. He decided to leave the hospital for good when he realized that his therapist there was planning to leave at the end of the summer.

For the fall and winter, Michael moved back to his parents' home. He spent the majority of his time playing the flute or listening to music. He also started to see his first therapist again. In January 1967, Michael's sister introduced him to a teacher named Betty, who also had some emotional difficulties. This was his first serious relationship, though he had had sex with a few women in Cambridge and lived with a young woman for a couple of months when he lived in New York City.

Tensions soon arose between Betty and Michael. His therapist was not happy with the relationship and discouraged Michael from pursuing it. Michael wanted to sleep with Betty, but she refused until she could be assured that they would have a lasting relationship. Michael was also considering returning to college and applied to Columbia University, but they rejected him. On Memorial Day weekend, Michael seemed to fall apart and wandered around the neighborhood playing his flute at all hours of the day.

Michael's therapist decided to hospitalize him again. Michael was now showing signs of paranoia; he was convinced that the FBI was watching him and that his mother was an FBI agent. At the hospital, a new therapist took over the case and, for the first time, Michael was diagnosed as schizophrenic. This new doctor arranged for Michael to go to another hospital that combined family therapy with insulin therapy. Betty visited Michael there but eventually stopped because of Michael's verbal abuse whenever she ventured an opinion about anything and because he hurt her by talking of liaisons that he was supposedly having with other women in the hospital.

Michael did not like the group family therapy sessions because they made him feel that the therapist was his parents' doctor rather than his. Some important material did come out in these sessions: Michael had considered pursuing a career in journalism but did not because he felt that his father would have resented it; and the fact that he had a physical attraction to his mother, an issue that had come up before. Michael finally agreed to have insulin therapy. He eventually participated more in the program at the hospital, helping with the more difficult patients and writing for the patients' newspaper, but he was frequently aloof and combative when his parents visited.

After three months, Michael's depression worsened, and he demanded to leave. Various things were bothering him; Betty had broken with him completely by this time, and one of his friends at the hospital had jumped to his death while on leave from the hospital. In late February, while home for a visit,

Michael insisted that he did not want to return to the hospital and tried to throw himself out of the window. His father restrained him.

This suicide attempt necessitated a 60-day commitment, after which time Michael was moved to a halfway house. At this time Michael was given electroconvulsive therapy, and his depression seemed to lessen. He also worked in an occupational therapy program. After release, Michael came home to a bleak life. He worked at the hospital every day but found it hard to establish a social life. He had dates with fellow workers and ex-patients and went to advertized "singles parties," but this did not alleviate his loneliness.

Michael met Vicky that spring, another ex-patient with whom he fell in love, but by the fall the relationship deteriorated. He obtained a job with a market research firm, but when business fell off, they reduced his hours.

Then, in September 1968, his therapist decided to move to another state. Michael switched to a psychoanalyst whose treatment style was very different from the family-style therapy that his previous therapist used.

In April 1969, a co-worker of Michael's called Michael's father to tell him that Michael was trying to buy a gun. Michael's father managed to get that information to his son's therapist, whom he thought would be discreet, but the therapist told Michael. Michael was angry about this and when he got home, he denied the accusation that he had tried to buy a gun.

By May, Michael was becoming more withdrawn, nervous and hostile. He seemed to be anxious about slipping once more into psychosis. Michael thought of contacting his previous therapist, but his father lied and told Michael that he did not know his new telephone number. Michael killed himself in his bedroom in his parents' apartment with an overdose of medication on the night of May 15. His parents found him the following morning. His suicide note said:

> Sorry, but one can't keep every promise. Don't blame yourselves, or anyone. Please don't let it hurt you. You must be together, and go on with each other. Mike.

Discussion

Michael was treated by eight different therapists over a period of nine years, as well as by interns and residents during the 26 months of hospitalization in five institutions.

Although Michael eventually received the diagnosis of schizophrenia, and he did show symptoms of paranoia toward the end of his life, his symptoms were more complex than that simple term implies. He suffered from obsessive fears and images, apprehension and shyness with women and premature ejaculation. He also had a fear that others thought he was a homosexual. Since Michael's father had limited contact with Michael's therapists and he wrote the book from which we derived all information about Michael, we are given no detailed exploration of the symptoms.

It is easy, therefore, to attribute Michael's suicide to the psychosis, and in particular to Michael's fear of continually slipping back into psychosis. He seemed to have been very discouraged by his failure to overcome his problems, and his inability to finish his undergraduate career depressed him profoundly.

His interpersonal life also caused him distress. Problems with Betty seemed to have precipitated a breakdown, and his suicide followed a period of conflict with Vicky.

However, what is missing in the story of his life is an analysis of what transpired between Michael and his parents. Michael was often angry at them and attributed his disturbance at least in part to them. His sexual attraction to his mother was discussed in a family therapy session, and his problems with women may have been related to this.

His anger was usually directed at his father, and his father wrote the story of his son's life with little insight into the role that he himself may have played. He admits that life at home was turbulent, but does not tell us how. He admits he was often away and was preoccupied with his career. He admits his interactions with Michael were often trite and superficial. And he makes it clear that he wanted to be involved with every therapist that Michael had. He seemed most content with the

therapists who let him participate in the sessions and extraor-
dinarily angry with the therapists who excluded him. Of
course, he was justifiably concerned about his son, but his
anger at the therapists seems inappropriate.

Mr. Wechsler wrote his book as a tribute to his son and as
a means of increasing awareness of mental illness. Wechsler
says that the main message is, however, for relatives of disturbed people "to resist being intimidated by professional
counsel and place some faith in their own instincts" (p. 14).
Perhaps Wechsler's need to lay the blame on the therapists for
his son's suicide obscures the true reasons for his son's psychosis and death.

COMMENT

The two case histories just described illustrate several important
features of suicide in youth, but they cannot by any means be
considered typical or wholly representative examples from which
general conclusions about suicidal behavior can be drawn. Quite
simply, there are no universal explanations for adolescent suicide.
Each suicide must be considered within the context of the individual adolescent and his family. Although no single cause for
suicide exists, nor is there a set of circumstances common to
adolescent suicides, certain recurrent themes often appear in the
histories of young people who kill themselves. These will become
apparent in subsequent chapters.

These particular case histories were selected mostly because they provide the reader with a reasonably full view of
the lives of two adolescents who committed suicide. Complete
case histories are usually hard to come by. Normally, clinicians
and scholars must look for pertinent information from many
different sources, and these sources may very well be of uncer-
tain reliability. In the above cases the histories are provided by
single, direct sources — the mother of one victim and the father
of the other. Although the parents' views are biased and therefore potentially flawed, this weakness may be less important

than the insight the parents give relative to family diagnosis — a key element in attempting to understand adolescent suicide.

In any event, it is clear from the two stories that manifestations of suicidal behavior in young people are very diverse (as will become more apparent throughout this book) and that the two cases have little in common. Jody White killed himself after rejection by a girlfriend, imitating his father's suicidal act years before. Michael Wechsler, on the other hand, killed himself after a long psychiatric illness — a reasonably common sequence in all suicides.

Could these suicides have been prevented? This issue is of primary concern to most of us. Although the psychodynamics of suicide are of keen interest, the clinician seeks predictive criteria above all. In these cases, Jody White committed suicide somewhat impulsively. This type of suicide is usually very difficult to predict, even though this young man's chances of committing suicide may have been considered somewhat elevated, not only because his father committed suicide, but also because Jody identified strongly with him. Michael Wechsler's suicide might have been somewhat easier to anticipate because of his prolonged psychiatric illness. The problem is that although the rate of suicide in those who are psychiatrically disturbed is higher than in non-psychiatrically disturbed people, most psychiatrically ill people do not die by suicide, but by natural causes. Furthermore, it is difficult to predict just when a such an individual will decide to take his life.

Clearly, there are many unanswered questions about adolescent suicide. Since findings of the existing literature are often conflicting, I have tried throughout this book to examine many sides of this problem.

REFERENCES

Wechsler, J.A. 1972. *In a Darkness*. New York: Norton.

White-Bowden, S. 1985. *Everything to Live For*. New York: Poseidon.

Chapter 2

The Incidence of Adolescent Suicide

There have been many community surveys of the incidence of suicidal preoccupation and suicide attempts among adolescents. For example, Dubow and co-workers (1989) found that among junior high school students, 36 percent had thought about suicide at some point in their lives and 7 percent had actually attempted suicide. A study of suicide ideation among high school students reported incidences of 53 percent and 8 percent respectively (Friedman et al. 1987). One study of *current* suicidal thoughts found an incidence of 7 percent, with the incidence increasing steadily from 8-year-olds to 17-year-olds (Kashani et al. 1989).

In their study of junior high school students, Dubow's team (1989) found that a history of suicidal preoccupation was more common in: (1) girls; (2) those from lower socioeconomic classes; (3) those with more stressful life experiences; (4) those who displayed less academic achievement; (5) those with less supportive families and (6) those who showed evidence of antisocial behavior.

Bolger's team (1989) asked students when they first thought about suicide and noted that the incidence sharply increased at age 11. Similarly, acts of attempted and completed suicide increase dramatically at puberty. There are several possible reasons for this. Young children may not have a mature concept of death, believing that it is temporary and reversible (Nagy 1948), and so their self-destructive behavior may not be truly suicidal. Additionally, hormonal levels increase at puberty, and several investigators have speculated that estrogens and androgens may play a role in the suicidal behavior of adolescents (Lester 1992). There may also be an increase in stressful life experiences during adolescence and this may precipitate suicidal preoccupation and behavior. Interestingly, Lester (1990) found that college students showed *less* suicidal preoccupation (and depression) than high school students in the same community, suggesting that stress levels may decrease after graduation from high school.

Gifted children seem to be as likely to report a history of suicidal preoccupation as regular students (Harkavy and Asnis 1985), but the mentally retarded show less involvement in suicidal behavior of high lethality, instead showing more self-mutilating behavior, which is not considered to be life-threatening (Kaminer et al. 1987).

Pfeffer and Trad (1988) do not agree that true suicidal behavior cannot be found in very young children. They documented that explicit suicidal threats and attempts can be found in children 3 to 6 years old. Rosenthal and Rosenthal (1984) showed that suicidal preschoolers were more often unwanted, abused and neglected than normal preschoolers, and they tended to run away from home more often. They also seemed to be less sensitive to pain and cried less than normal preschoolers.

METHODS FOR COMPLETED SUICIDE

In America in 1980, the most common methods used by adult men for committing suicide were firearms (64 percent) and hanging (15 percent), whereas for adult women the most common methods were firearms (40 percent) and poisons and overdoses (26 percent). The same was true for those aged 15 to

24. Young men used firearms (64 percent) and hanging (18 percent), whereas young women used firearms (53 percent) and poisons and overdoses (20 percent).

SEX DIFFERENCES

In general, in almost every country in the world, men kill themselves more often than women do. Women attempt suicide (but survive) more than men do. In the Netherlands in 1970 and 1971, De Graaf and Kruyt (1976) identified 731 male and 478 female completed suicides and 1562 male and 2551 female attempted suicides. (There has been no recent study like this in America, but a study in the 1950s in Los Angeles found this same difference.)

We have little idea of why there might be this sex difference (Lester 1984). One obvious difference is that the methods that men choose are more lethal (the probability of dying is greater). In a study in New Zealand, Langley and Johnston (1990) found that the success rate (i.e., death) for the various ways of committing suicide was:

hanging	88%
firearms	83%
car exhaust	78%
drowning	76%
jumping	60%
cooking gas	33%
cutting	10%
meds/poisons	2%

Women are more likely to use overdoses and cutting as a means of suicide than men (and so survive more), while men use firearms and hanging more than women (and so die more).

A similar difference in choice of method for suicide is found in adolescents. For example, in Canada, boys use guns more often for suicide than do girls (Tonkin 1984) and in the United States boys use hanging more than do girls (Peck 1987).

Younger children are more likely to use less lethal methods, such as running out into traffic (Husain and Vandiver 1984).

Another possible reason that males and females commit suicide in different ways is that people are aware of this sex difference in suicidal behavior, and so social expectations about what is "masculine" and what is "feminine" behavior are learned.

THE TIMING OF THE SUICIDAL ACT

In America, completed suicide among adults is most common in the spring (with a minor peak in the fall) and on Mondays (Lester 1992). Suicide rates are lower on the major national holidays.

Adolescents and youths do not show these seasonal or daily variations when they choose to commit suicide. The seasonal peak is much weaker in the young (those aged 15 to 24) and, if it occurs, is found in fall or winter (Lester 1992). The suicide rate of youths is highest on Sundays rather than Mondays, but again the variation by day is weaker in the young; and the young do not show a decrease in the suicide rate on the major national holidays.

CONCLUSIONS

The lifetime incidence of suicidal thoughts is remarkably high in adolescents, with over 50 percent of high school students reporting that they have thought about suicide at some point in their lives. Roughly 7 percent report that they currently think about suicide. This preoccupation with suicide is not merely intellectual since almost 10 percent of high school students have made a suicide attempt.

Looking at lethal suicidal actions, adolescents and youths use the same methods as adults and, by 1980, guns were the preferred method for both sexes (whereas in the 1950s the preferred method for women was overdoses and poison). Although it may be impossible to implement such an action, many commentators have suggested that restricting the availability of guns in America might reduce the suicide rate of both the young and the old (Clarke and Lester 1989).

REFERENCES

Bolger, N., G. Downey, E. Walker and P. Steininger. 1989. The onset of suicidal ideation in childhood and adolescence. *Journal of Youth and Adolescence* 18:175-190.

Clarke, R.V. and D. Lester. 1989. *Suicide: Closing the Exits*. New York: Springer-Verlag.

Dubow, E.F., D.F. Kausch, M.C. Blum and J. Reed. 1989. Correlates of suicidal ideation and attempts in a community sample of junior high school students. *Journal of Clinical Child Psychology* 18:158-166.

De Graaf, A.C. and C.S. Kruyt. 1976. Some results of the response to a national survey of suicide and attempted suicide in the Netherlands. In *Suicide and Attempted Suicide in Young People*. Copenhagen: World Health Organization.

Friedman, J.M., G.M. Asnis, M. Boeck and J. DiFore. 1987. Prevalence of specific suicidal behaviors in a high school sample. *American Journal of Psychiatry* 144: 1203-1206.

Harkavy, J.M. and G. Asnis. 1985. Suicide attempts in adolescence. *New England Journal of Medicine* 313:1290-1291.

Husain, S.A. and T. Vandiver. 1984. *Suicide in Children and Adolescents*. New York: Spectrum.

Kaminer, Y., C. Feinstein and R. Barrett. 1987. Suicidal behavior in mentally retarded adolescents. *Child Psychiatry and Human Development* 18(2):90-94.

Kashani, J.H., P. Goddard and J.C. Reid. 1989. Correlates of suicidal ideation in a community sample of children and adolescents. *Journal of the American Academy of Child and Adolescent Psychiatry* 28:912-917.

Langley, J.D. and S.E. Johnston. 1990. Purposely self-inflicted injury resulting in death and hospitalization in New Zealand. *Community Health Studies* 14:190-199.

Lester, D. Suicide. 1984. In C.S. Widom, ed., *Sex Roles and Psychopathology*. New York: Plenum.

Lester, D. 1990. Depression and suicide in college students and adolescents. *Personality and Individual Differences* 11:757-758.

Lester, D. 1992. *Why People Kill Themselves*. Springfield, IL: Charles C Thomas.

Nagy, M. 1948. The child's theories concerning death. *Journal of Genetic Psychology* 73:3-27.

Peck, D. 1987. Socio-psychological correlates of adolescent and youthful suicide. *Adolescence* 22:863-878.

Pfeffer, C. and P.V. Trad. 1988. Sadness and suicidal tendencies in preschool children. *Journal of Developmental and Behavioral Pediatrics* 9(2):86-88.

Rosenthal, P. and S. Rosenthal. 1984. Suicidal behavior by preschool children. *American Journal of Psychiatry* 141:520-525.

Smith, K. and S. Crawford. 1986. Suicidal behavior among normal high school students. *Suicide and Life-Threatening Behavior* 16:313-325.

Tonkin, R.S. 1984. Suicide methods in British Columbia adolescents. *Journal of Adolescent Health Care* 5:172-177.

Chapter 3

Youth Suicide Around the World

As discussed in the previous chapter, one of the most striking epidemiologic features of suicide in America is the rising rate of suicide among youths (ages 15-24) in recent years. This chapter will explore the extent of this trend in other nations.

Scholars sometimes believe that the data that they have derived from their own nation are typical of all nations at all times, but this belief is not always valid. A cross-cultural perspective will help identify which aspects of a phenomenon are unique to the nation in which it was first identified and which aspects have applicability beyond that specific region.

YOUTH SUICIDE RATES IN OTHER NATIONS

Lester (1988) examined the changes from 1970 to 1980 in the suicide rates of youths in various nations of the world. His data, reproduced in Table 3-1, show the great variation among nations of the world in the changes in youth suicide. (The suicide rates of each different nation are reported to the World Health

Organization only for 10-year age groups; therefore, the youth suicide rates listed in Table 3-1 are for those aged 15-24.)

Table 3-1.

Suicide Rates in 1970 (per 100,000 per year) and Changes by 1980 for the Total Population and for Those Aged 15-24

	Total Population		*Youth*	
	1970	*% change by 1980*	*1970*	*% change by 1980*
Australia	12.4	-11.2%	8.6	+ 30.2%
Austria	24.2	+ 6.2%	16.5	+ 9.1%
Bulgaria	11.9	+ 14.3%	6.9	+ 34.8%
Canada	11.3	+ 23.9%	10.2	+ 50.0%
Chile	6.0	-18.3%	10.1	-31.7%
Denmark	21.5	+ 47.0%	8.5	+ 42.4%
Finland	21.3	+ 20.7%	14.7	+ 60.5%
France	15.4	+ 26.0%	7.0	+ 52.9%
Greece	3.2	+ 3.1%	1.5	+ 20.0%
Hong Kong	13.6	-0.7%	7.7	+ 1.3%
Hungary	34.8	+ 29.0%	18.9	+ 5.8%
Italy	5.8	+ 25.9%	2.9	+ 34.5%
Japan	15.2	+ 15.8%	13.0	-3.8%
Netherlands	8.1	+ 24.7%	4.0	+ 50.0%
New Zealand	9.6	+ 12.5%	8.0	+ 73.7%
Norway	8.4	+ 47.6%	3.7	+ 224.3%
Portugal	7.5	-1.3%	4.5	+ 2.2%
Singapore	8.9	+ 25.8%	7.8	+ 32.1%
Spain	4.2	+ 4.8%	1.4	+ 92.9%
Sweden	22.3	-13.0%	13.3	-13.5%
Switzerland	18.6	+ 38.2%	13.0	+ 80.0%
Thailand	4.2	+ 76.2%	7.2	+ 77.8%
UK: England & Wales	8.0	+ 10.0%	6.0	+ 6.7%
UK: Scotland	7.6	+ 31.6%	5.8	+ 65.5%
USA	11.5	+ 2.6%	8.8	+ 39.8%
Venezuela	6.8	-23.5%	14.5	-28.3%
West Germany	21.3	-1.9%	13.4	-6.7%

The nations with the most increase in youth suicide rates were Norway (+ 224%), Spain (+ 93%), Switzerland (+ 80%) and Thailand (+ 78%). New Zealand, Finland, Canada and the Netherlands also experienced large increases from 1970 to 1980. In contrast, several nations witnessed decreases, including Chile (-32%), Venezuela (-28%), and Sweden (-13%). West Germany and Japan also experienced decreases during this period.

A close look reveals that many nations experienced an increase in total suicide rates among all ages. This rise also varied with gender. Thus, it makes sense to compare the increase in youth suicide rates with the suicide rates of the total population.

Using the criterion that the percentage increase in the youth suicide rate must be at least 10 percent of the percentage increase in the overall suicide rates, the following nations showed a rise in youth suicide rates in both males and females: Finland, the Netherlands, New Zealand, Norway, Scotland, Spain and Switzerland. Nations with a rising youth suicide rate in males only were: Australia, Canada, France, Greece, Italy, Thailand and the United States. Nations with a rising youth suicide rate in females only were: Austria, Bulgaria, England and Wales and Singapore.

It is clear that during these years there was no universal pattern. Different nations experienced very different changes in the rate of youth suicide — both male and female — compared to the suicide rate of the total population.

Lester examined the association between various social indicators and youth suicide rates and found that the associations for youth suicide rates were sometimes different than those for non-youth suicide rates. For example, Lester found that the overall suicide rate was greater in nations with a higher quality of life, but youth suicides did not seem to be at all related to the quality of life. In addition, the overall suicide rate rose more from 1970 to 1980 in nations that had higher suicide rates in 1970, but this was not true for youth suicide rates. Lester confessed that he was puzzled; his studies on the suicide rate of youths identified fewer correlates (and, therefore, fewer possible explanatory factors) than for the overall suicide rate.

Youth suicide is clearly harder to categorize and, therefore, understand than adult suicide.

Because many nations do not consider suicide a possibility for children, officially reported suicides for those aged 5-14 are not as reliable as those for older youths. (As stated above, it could be argued that children do not have a mature concept of death and, therefore, could not be consciously seeking death when they attempt to, or actually do, commit suicide.) Ignoring such objections, Barraclough (1987) examined the officially reported suicide rates of those aged 5-14 and found that the female suicide rates were as high or higher than the male rates in 14 nations, mainly in South America and Asia. This is surprising and noteworthy since the overall male suicide rates are higher than female suicide rates in almost all nations of the world.

THE PEAK SUICIDE RATE

Rates of suicide by age are shown in Table 3-2 for several nations of the world in 1970 and 1980 (with updates for 1988 for nations where data were available). Some nations, such as Austria and Greece, have suicide rates that rise consistently from ages 15-24 to 75 and older. In some of these nations, the age for those who commit suicide is 75 and older. For example, in Hungary the suicide rate for men aged 75+ in 1980 was 202.2 per 100,000 per year compared to 31.5 for men aged 15-24. The rate for elderly men was double that in Bulgaria and Singapore, the nations with the next highest rates of suicide for that age group.

Three nations showed the peak suicide rate for women in the 15 to 24 year-old age range: Chile, Thailand and Venezuela. Perhaps the fact that these three nations are relatively poor is an indication that less developed nations have peak rates of suicides for young women.

Several nations have peak suicide rates in middle-age groups. For example, the peak suicide rate for Australian women was in those aged 55-64 in 1970 and in those aged 35-44 in 1980.

Table 3-2.

Suicide Rates by Age in Countries of the World in 1970, 1980 and (where available) 1988

Ages	15-24	25-34	35-44	45-54	55-64	65-74	75+
Australia							
1970 male	12.4	20.1	26.1	33.6	30.9	31.9	38.5
1980 male	17.6	22.9	23.4	22.3	24.0	22.4	31.9
1988 male	27.8	28.2	26.0	24.4	23.8	27.7	39.8
1970 female	4.7	7.8	11.8	14.6	17.0	14.4	9.5
1980 female	4.5	6.9	9.8	9.2	7.9	7.1	9.1
1988 female	4.5	7.2	7.5	8.2	8.7	7.4	10.0
Austria							
1970 male	27.0	31.7	46.6	58.5	64.6	72.7	77.7
1980 male	28.8	36.3	43.9	59.3	56.3	72.6	85.7
1988 male	27.2	38.6	42.2	48.1	47.6	58.6	107.5
1970 female	5.7	8.2	16.4	22.3	25.7	27.6	29.4
1980 female	6.7	11.1	14.3	20.7	23.0	29.1	33.9
1988 female	4.7	10.3	13.6	16.5	22.5	22.9	29.7
Bulgaria							
1970 male	9.0	11.6	11.3	19.3	27.1	53.2	108.3
1980 male	11.1	12.9	16.3	21.9	26.8	52.2	108.7
1988 male	12.5	15.7	21.8	25.6	33.7	51.2	118.1
1970 female	4.8	4.9	5.3	9.8	15.9	18.4	34.5
1980 female	7.4	5.8	5.7	8.2	14.4	17.0	31.9
1988 female	6.2	6.3	4.1	9.5	14.3	21.6	42.3
Canada							
1970 male	15.6	20.1	26.6	27.9	31.9	28.0	24.6
1980 male	24.8	29.5	25.1	30.7	28.5	26.9	38.1
1988 male	26.9	29.2	26.1	24.2	28.0	26.2	30.6
1970 female	4.8	8.6	10.6	14.5	11.4	9.5	4.6
1980 female	5.4	8.1	8.8	13.7	12.1	9.5	5.9
1988 female	4.9	7.1	9.8	9.9	6.9	6.1	6.2
Chile							
1970 male	14.3	17.7	14.9	16.6	13.9	22.1	19.9

Ages	15-24	25-34	35-44	45-54	55-64	65-74	75+
1980 male	10.8	12.1	13.9	12.5	15.3	10.6	21.2
1970 female	6.1	3.4	1.6	3.2	2.9	3.0	3.5
1980 female	2.9	1.9	0.9	1.7	2.9	1.3	2.4
Denmark							
1970 male	11.1	25.4	39.5	55.9	48.8	45.7	55.0
1980 male	16.3	42.7	61.8	70.7	71.8	60.4	81.3
1988 male	15.9	33.6	44.7	50.5	52.6	47.2	69.2
1970 female	5.7	10.6	22.6	30.2	34.1	26.7	19.1
1980 female	7.7	16.7	35.8	42.8	39.3	32.9	31.6
1988 female	5.5	12.0	20.6	33.2	33.2	36.0	33.1
Finland							
1970 male	22.5	41.5	55.8	60.9	62.6	66.5	50.5
1980 male	37.5	55.7	55.0	60.3	54.9	62.1	60.1
1988 male	39.6	60.4	65.8	64.4	54.7	60.3	65.6
1970 female	6.7	9.4	11.2	20.6	15.9	12.2	7.4
1980 female	9.1	9.5	11.4	16.8	16.2	22.8	9.7
1988 female	7.5	7.7	13.2	25.4	18.3	16.9	14.4
France							
1970 male	9.4	17.1	25.5	36.2	51.1	55.3	74.4
1980 male	15.7	27.4	32.7	39.7	41.2	57.1	99.6
1988 male	13.9	32.5	38.2	40.0	41.2	47.5	109.0
1970 female	4.4	7.4	8.0	11.3	16.3	17.9	18.6
1980 female	5.4	9.6	13.2	14.9	17.2	22.6	24.4
1988 female	4.2	9.0	12.7	19.8	17.6	22.9	25.3
Greece							
1970 male	1.7	3.9	6.1	6.7	10.6	10.7	11.6
1980 male	3.0	5.4	5.6	5.2	5.4	10.1	16.6
1988 male	4.8	7.4	5.7	5.9	9.9	7.5	17.5
1970 female	1.4	1.7	1.0	3.2	4.3	1.7	5.6
1980 female	0.6	1.1	1.9	2.8	2.9	4.5	6.1
1988 female	0.6	1.6	1.5	2.9	3.3	6.9	6.0
Hong Kong							
1970 male	7.2	27.3	23.8	33.8	41.5	50.5	88.7
1980 male	7.9	18.7	17.2	27.6	31.4	53.8	63.0

Ages	15-24	25-34	35-44	45-54	55-64	65-74	75+
1970 female	8.2	11.1	18.9	13.2	26.8	46.4	89.1
1980 female	7.6	12.4	11.8	14.3	21.4	44.4	64.6
Hungary							
1970 male	27.8	48.6	63.6	78.4	85.1	104.9	146.4
1980 male	31.5	58.3	86.8	106.4	96.7	116.3	202.2
1988 male	21.0	57.8	79.4	99.7	84.8	96.0	172.9
1970 female	9.6	11.0	17.5	23.8	33.8	46.2	76.4
1980 female	8.0	16.4	26.7	36.2	42.2	52.9	90.6
1988 female	10.1	19.0	27.2	34.8	35.9	46.8	74.9
Italy							
1970 male	3.5	5.9	7.4	11.4	18.3	24.3	33.3
1980 male	5.3	8.3	9.1	14.0	17.3	26.5	37.4
1988 male	4.9	9.1	9.9	12.1	16.2	28.3	47.4
1970 female	2.3	2.7	3.5	5.2	7.0	7.5	7.8
1980 female	2.4	3.3	4.2	6.8	8.2	10.2	10.2
1988 female	1.4	2.7	3.6	5.7	7.3	9.7	11.1
Japan							
1970 male	14.0	20.1	17.8	20.1	32.3	50.4	82.1
1980 male	16.6	24.9	28.9	33.3	32.2	40.9	73.3
1988 male	10.4	21.9	26.6	41.2	37.8	39.2	72.2
1970 female	11.9	13.8	10.0	13.5	20.6	40.5	66.3
1980 female	8.2	11.4	12.5	15.1	17.8	35.5	60.2
1988 female	6.5	9.3	10.4	16.6	19.3	30.6	54.9
Netherlands							
1970 male	5.8	6.4	11.1	15.7	24.0	25.4	42.5
1980 male	8.3	14.9	15.1	17.1	22.3	26.1	41.1
1988 male	8.2	16.1	14.3	17.2	20.0	21.2	41.3
1970 female	2.1	5.5	7.5	11.0	12.6	14.9	17.5
1980 female	3.7	8.0	8.9	12.4	14.1	14.3	12.0
1988 female	2.4	8.3	9.3	11.2	14.0	13.1	10.7
New Zealand							
1970 male	12.1	10.4	23.1	24.5	16.8	34.6	31.2
1980 male	19.5	17.8	17.4	17.3	22.2	24.4	35.6
1970 female	0.0	3.8	2.9	8.5	12.1	21.1	19.2
1980 female	0.0	8.1	9.3	6.8	15.6	4.4	13.1

Ages	15-24	25-34	35-44	45-54	55-64	65-74	75 +
Norway							
1970 male	5.4	15.0	17.4	19.2	24.7	19.6	13.3
1980 male	20.4	18.2	20.6	28.6	31.8	25.5	24.0
1988 male	26.6	31.4	27.5	36.8	34.4	25.4	33.7
1970 female	2.0	4.5	10.1	10.4	8.9	6.9	1.9
1980 female	3.3	9.0	6.7	14.2	12.1	9.6	4.7
1988 female	6.5	11.7	13.8	14.3	13.1	13.0	7.7
Portugal							
1970 male	5.6	6.2	17.5	14.5	27.6	43.4	72.2
1980 male	5.2	7.9	14.7	18.6	24.1	31.0	53.7
1988 male	6.4	8.7	10.7	20.0	23.2	33.4	49.2
1970 female	3.6	2.1	3.0	3.8	6.7	9.2	11.7
1980 female	4.1	5.4	3.8	4.2	5.4	5.6	11.0
1988 female	2.9	2.7	1.8	4.5	5.4	10.2	9.3
Singapore							
1970 male	9.1	8.1	13.3	23.2	39.0	56.5	137.9
1980 male	9.0	17.7	8.1	17.5	32.9	40.9	107.4
1970 female	6.3	15.7	0.0	14.1	14.5	39.9	53.6
1980 female	11.7	10.1	8.3	12.3	17.1	34.5	57.3
Spain							
1970 male	2.0	4.1	7.0	9.6	15.7	21.9	29.0
1980 male	4.3	6.2	6.6	9.7	12.4	18.6	28.5
1970 female	0.9	1.4	1.6	3.8	5.4	5.7	6.9
1980 female	1.1	1.3	2.1	3.3	4.9	4.7	6.4
Sweden							
1970 male	18.5	27.9	44.9	52.5	54.6	46.3	48.8
1980 male	16.9	33.3	37.6	43.9	35.3	39.3	48.9
1970 female	7.9	15.3	19.3	26.0	17.8	15.6	13.0
1980 female	5.8	11.3	16.2	17.8	21.2	14.5	11.4
Switzerland							
1970 male	21.3	27.6	31.2	46.2	49.0	49.5	74.1
1980 male	34.2	36.5	42.2	46.1	63.4	58.9	80.7
1988 male	26.3	38.0	36.6	39.6	41.7	48.5	74.8

Ages	15-24	25-34	35-44	45-54	55-64	65-74	75+
1970 female	4.7	10.2	8.8	19.5	19.1	21.7	16.0
1980 female	12.3	14.8	17.6	21.7	20.8	26.8	23.2
1988 female	7.1	10.0	13.7	17.5	19.7	22.2	26.4
Thailand							
1970 male	7.2	5.7	9.0	8.5	11.7	9.5	10.7
1980 male	12.8	11.1	11.6	13.8	12.9	12.6	(65+)
1970 female	9.9	3.4	3.8	3.0	2.8	2.2	1.1
1980 female	19.6	8.6	7.4	7.1	4.8	3.3	(65+)
UK: England							
and Wales							
1970 male	6.0	9.1	11.3	14.1	17.5	20.7	23.9
1980 male	6.4	13.0	15.5	15.4	17.9	18.2	21.6
1988 male	11.0	15.5	18.0	14.7	15.3	16.2	24.3
1970 female	2.6	4.4	7.4	10.3	12.9	15.3	9.7
1980 female	3.0	4.2	8.1	10.9	11.8	13.3	11.0
1988 female	2.5	3.8	4.9	6.4	6.8	8.0	8.4
UK: Scotland							
1970 male	5.8	8.6	15.6	13.1	24.0	12.9	21.7
1980 male	9.6	15.2	19.1	23.4	17.8	18.8	23.2
1988 male	20.5	23.9	22.5	26.6	18.8	12.9	24.1
1970 female	1.8	5.8	8.2	15.1	12.7	5.7	5.6
1980 female	3.1	7.0	9.6	14.3	14.3	10.9	8.1
1988 female	4.9	7.7	9.8	7.9	7.7	12.0	6.0
USA							
1970 male	13.5	19.6	22.2	27.8	32.8	36.5	41.8
1980 male	20.2	24.8	22.3	23.0	24.4	30.2	43.5
1988 male	21.9	25.0	22.9	21.7	25.0	33.0	57.8
1970 female	4.2	8.6	12.1	12.5	11.4	9.3	6.7
1980 female	4.3	7.0	8.4	9.4	8.4	6.5	5.4
1988 female	4.2	5.7	6.9	7.9	7.2	6.8	6.4
Venezuela							
1970 male	14.5	12.6	17.8	19.0	28.8	42.5	47.5
1980 male	10.4	13.9	13.1	18.5	20.6	24.9	46.8
1970 female	11.3	5.6	4.1	4.1	3.0	7.6	5.3
1980 female	3.5	3.2	3.3	2.8	2.4	1.8	2.8

Ages	15-24	25-34	35-44	45-54	55-64	65-74	75+
West Germany							
1970 male	19.6	27.0	35.1	43.2	51.6	53.9	75.2
1980 male	19.0	26.9	33.0	42.0	38.9	54.0	72.8
1988 male	15.8	22.7	24.4	33.0	35.5	41.3	77.8
1970 female	6.9	11.5	15.9	25.4	27.2	26.1	27.0
1980 female	5.6	9.9	14.0	20.4	23.6	27.1	25.9
1988 female	4.7	7.7	9.5	13.6	14.6	19.5	24.1

DISCUSSION

Our aim in this chapter was to bring an international perspective to the problem of youth suicide. The data presented indicated that the rising youth suicide rate was not found in every nation of the world. Some nations experienced a decrease in the youth suicide rate, while others are witnessing a rise in the youth suicide rate in only one sex. Unfortunately, scholars are unable at the present time to explain these differences. They represent part of the enigma of suicide in youth.

REFERENCES

Barraclough, B.M. 1987. Sex ratio of juvenile suicide. *Journal of the American Academy of Child and Adolescent Psychiatry* 26:434-435.

Lester, D. 1988. Youth suicide: a cross-cultural perspective. *Adolescence* 23:955-958.

Chapter 4

The Suicidal Act

The most common question asked when someone commits suicide is, "Why did he do it?" The most obvious answer is to look for signs of any precipitating stress. "Did he just break up with his girlfriend?" "Was he having a problem with his schoolwork?"

The problem with this kind of answer is that many people experience stressors, but only a very small percentage kill themselves as a result. If the breakup of a relationship frequently led to suicide, almost half of adult Americans (i.e., those who have divorced) would have committed suicide! Most of those who lose a loved one, who experience loss of their job, who suffer from a terminal illness, or who live through famine or war die natural deaths.

Nevertheless, there are some interesting features of stress associated with suicide. In general, both completed and attempted adult suicides show higher levels of *recent* stressful life experiences than nonsuicidal people. The same appears to be true for suicidal adolescents and young adults.

For example, compared to nonsuicidal adolescents, suicidal adolescents seem to have experienced more recent stress, particularly stress from their families (Pomerantz and Carter 1987). They are also more likely to have a family member who is depressed or suicidal, to have been the victim of violence or to have witnessed violence within the family, to have experienced the death of a sibling or friend, or to have their divorced parents remarry.

This finding of an increase in overall stress, and sometimes in specific sources of stress, has been replicated by many other researchers. Cohen-Sandler and his team (1982) found that this increase was significant when recent, but not when it went back to infancy, preschool years or early childhood.

AGE DIFFERENCES

There are differences in the precipitants of suicide and the type of recent stress between young and old suicides. For example, young completed suicides in one study were found to have experienced even higher levels of recent stress, including the past week, than the older suicides (Rich et al. 1986). They had experienced less stress from illness but more stress from interpersonal loss and conflict. The younger suicides experienced more legal troubles and they were more often unemployed. They were also more likely to be drug abusers.

Eisele and his colleagues (1987) found that for adolescent completed suicides family and school were more often precipitants of their suicidal actions, in contrast to adults whose reasons for suicide were more often the result of stress from mental and physical illnesses.

Very young children often act deviantly in response to conscious or unconscious desires of their parents (a possibility discussed in greater detail in Chapter 6). Supporting this idea, Husain and Vandiver (1984) found that children below the age of 15 were suicidal more often as a result of rejection or hostility toward them, particularly hostility from parents and siblings, compared to those in their late teens who were more likely to be suicidal as a reaction to depression.

The Suicide Note

Completed suicides leave very little for researchers to study, but one item that is often present is the suicide note, left by about 40 percent of all suicides. Several analyses of the contents of suicide notes confirm the difference in the precipitants of suicide for adolescents and adults.

Several studies have found that the suicide notes left by young people contain more anger, more self-blame and even malicious content than the suicide notes left by older people, which more frequently express the wish to die, the wish to escape from psychological and physical pain and suffering (Farberow and Shneidman 1957). Notes left by older people tend to give instructions and are often rather unemotional (Tuckman et al. 1959; Capstick 1960). The suicide notes left by young people more often blame others for their troubles (Peck 1980-81).

Leenaars (1989) found that the suicide notes left by young people gave evidence of more disturbed interpersonal relationships, less ability to adjust to difficulties, more ambivalence, the possible involvement of unconscious motives, and more identification with someone who has either rejected the note writer or who has been lost (through desertion or death) than suicide notes left by older people.

REPEAT SUICIDE ATTEMPTS

It has long been noted that a fair proportion of suicide attempters make *repeated* nonlethal attempts. It should not be thought that repeaters are less intent on suicide than non-repeaters. In fact, Farmer and Creed (1986) found that they had more suicidal intent. How do repeaters differ from non-repeaters?

Davidson and Choquet (1978) found that young repeaters were less educated, more often unemployed and also had more difficulty at school than first-time attempters. Their parents were more often alcohol abusers, hostile or indifferent to their children, as well as being more domineering. Repeaters were also more psychiatrically disturbed. Gispert and his team (1987) found that adolescent repeaters were less successful at school and truant more often, were more depressed and hostile, and had experienced more stressful life experiences.

Lester (1987) concluded that repeaters were more deviant in general than first-time attempters. They were more often psychiatrically disturbed, more often delinquents, and perhaps less well socialized than first-timers.

DISCUSSION

The existence of a great deal of recent stress is one of the four areas that are thought crucial to explore for an accurate evaluation of suicidal risk (the others are: psychiatric state, suicidal preoccupation and the behavior of significant others). We have seen that suicidal adolescents, like suicidal adults, are found to have experienced high levels and increased levels of stress prior to their suicidal actions. With adolescents, we must remember that the stressful nature of their experiences must not be judged by adult standards, but rather by their own subjective reactions to the experiences.

The suicide notes left by adolescent suicides show a much greater focus on interpersonal crises, whereas the suicide notes of older people show a much greater focus on internal (intra-psychic) problems.

Although some adolescents make repeated nonlethal attempts at suicide, such behavior must not be dismissed as non-life-threatening. Those who make repeated attempts at suicide have a much higher risk of killing themselves than those who do not make suicide attempts. The difficulty we face is in predicting exactly *when* the lethal suicidal act will occur. Rather than ignoring their actions, we should err on the side of overreaction, for only then might we save a life.

REFERENCES

Capstick, A. 1960. The recognition of emotional disturbance and the prevention of suicide. *British Medical Journal* 1:1179-1182.

Cohen-Sandler, R., A. Berman and R. King. 1982. Life stress and symptomatology. *Journal of the American Academy of Child Psychiatry* 21:178-186.

Davidson, F. and M. Choquet. 1978. Identification of factors of risk which are predictive of repeated suicide. In V. Aalberg, ed., *Proceedings of the Ninth International Congress for Suicide Prevention*. Helsinki: Finnish Association for Mental Health.

Eisele, J.W., J. Frisino, W. Haglund and D.T. Reay. 1987. Teenage suicide in King County, Washington. *American Journal of Forensic Medicine and Pathology* 8:208-216.

Farberow, N.L. and E.S. Shneidman. 1957. Suicide and Age. In E.S. Shneidman and N.L. Farberow, eds., *Clues to Suicide*. New York: McGraw-Hill.

Farmer, R. and F. Creed. 1986. Hostility and deliberate self-poisoning. *British Journal of Medical Psychology* 59:311-316.

Gispert, M., M. Davis, L. Marsh, and K. Wheeler. 1987. Predictive factors in repeated suicide attempts by adolescents. *Hospital and Community Psychiatry* 38:390-393.

Husain, S.A. and T. Vandiver. 1984. *Suicide in Children and Adolescents*. New York: Spectrum.

Leenaars, A.A. 1989. Are young adults' suicides psychologically different from those of older adults? *Suicide and Life-Threatening Behavior* 19:249-263.

Lester, D. 1987. *Suicide as a Learned Behavior*. Springfield, IL: Charles C Thomas.

Peck, D. 1980-81. Towards a theory of suicide. *Omega* 11:1-14.

Pomerantz, S.C. and B.F. Carter. 1987. Troubled youth. In R. Yufit, ed., *Proceedings of the 20th Annual Conference.* Denver: American Association of Suicidology.

Rich, C.L., D. Young and R.C. Fowler. 1986. San Diego suicide study. *Archives of General Psychiatry* 43:577-582.

Tuckman, J., R.J. Kleiner and M. Lavell. 1959. Emotional content of suicide notes. *American Journal of Psychiatry* 116:59-63.

Chapter 5

Psychiatric Illness and Adolescent Suicide

One of the most established facts in suicide research is that those with a psychiatric disorder have higher suicide rates than those who do not have such disorders. A history of psychiatric disturbance increases a person's likelihood of committing suicide from about 1.5 percent of all deaths in normal people to 15 percent of all deaths of those diagnosed with an affective or major depressive disorder.

This is not to say that all suicides are disturbed. Far from it. Although some investigators believe that all people who kill themselves are disturbed, a sampling of various studies finds that estimates of the percentage of suicides who are judged to be disturbed range from 5 percent to 94 percent (Temoche et al. 1964). The problem with this type of research is that the psychiatric evaluation has to be made after the person's death, and so the only sources of information about the suicides are observations made by their family, friends and co-workers. I have not found a study that tried the same evaluation with a comparison group of people who died of heart attacks, for example, so that we would have a comparison set of data.

Retrospective diagnoses are also incapable of being objective because they are never made without knowledge of the cause of the death; the psychiatrist knows that the deceased is a suicide, and this knowledge may affect the judgments of a psychiatrist who believes that those who kill themselves must be crazy.

For adults in general the rule is the more severe the psychiatric disorder, the higher the rate of suicides. Psychotics have higher rates of suicide than neurotics, who in turn have higher rates of suicide than those with personality disorders. Among psychotics, those with a major depressive disorder, whether unipolar or bipolar, have a slightly higher rate of suicide than those with schizophrenia.

These facts apply to adolescents as well. Asarnow and Guthrie (1989) found that adolescents who had attempted suicide were more often diagnosed as having a major depressive disorder than were nonsuicidal psychiatric patients. However, adolescent suicides differ to some degree from the general pattern found in adult suicides in that personality disorders are quite common. A personality disorder is a chronic maladaptive life style and there are several variants, such as borderline and antisocial personality disorders, that seem to be especially common in adolescent suicides.

For example, in a study of adolescent psychiatric inpatients, Apter and his colleagues (1988) found that suicidal preoccupation was most serious in adolescents who had a conduct disorder (that is, their behavior seemed undercontrolled and in turn caused them problems), less serious in those with major depressive disorders and least serious in those who were schizophrenic.

Depression is a psychiatric illness, but it also refers to a group of symptoms. Beck and his collaborators (1974) found that one of these symptoms — the cognitive state of feeling hopeless about the future — is more strongly associated with past, current and future suicidal behavior than others. Several investigators have found this to be true of suicidal adolescents, too. Cole (1989), for example, found that suicidal preoccupation was associated with hopelessness in high school students even after differences in the level of depression were taken into account and controlled for.

Psychiatric patients sometimes kill themselves in a deviant manner (compared to other suicides). Although they are disturbed and therefore known to be at higher risk of suicide, the timing of their suicidal act is slightly less predictable because of the influence of the psychotic symptoms (such as hallucinations and delusions and difficulties in communicating thoughts and feelings). Psychotics are also more likely to kill themselves using bizarre methods, such as self-immolation, or to jump to their deaths from buildings or in front of moving trains. This increased use of jumping by severely disturbed people may be a result of the lack of available lethal methods or deficiencies in their ability to plan more complicated suicidal actions.

Other psychiatric problems are also associated with an increase of the rate of suicide in adolescents, including alcohol and drug abuse and eating disorders (both anorexia and bulimia), behaviors that in themselves are quite self-destructive.

The life and suicide of Michael Wechsler, presented in the first chapter of this book, describes the life course of a psychiatrically disturbed young man. In this chapter, we will describe the life and death of another disturbed young man who killed himself.

CHRISTOPHER

Christopher Jens was born on February 24, 1944, the second of three sons. He killed himself on May 10, 1970, when he was 26 years old. His mother wrote his biography, including in her book many letters written to him and by him (Jens 1987). Compared to biographies written by those unrelated to the person who committed suicide, the information in this kind of biography is often not as objective and complete as it might be; the same is true of Wechsler's biography of his son. Chris's mother was interested in popular variants of psychological theory, particularly Jungian ideas, to an obsessive degree. This too colors her writing, but nonetheless her book provides some clues to the reasons for her son's suicide.

Chris's Parents

In 1943, the year before she gave birth to Chris, his mother sought psychiatric help. She had suicidal and sometimes homicidal thoughts and seemed to be unhappily married. She was trying to free herself from neurosis by reading books on psychology such as those written by Karen Horney. She describes herself as having phobias and obsessions at the time, but does not specify what they were. Her psychiatrist told her that it would be fine for her to have another child.

Chris had an uneventful birth and childhood, except for two bouts of very painful pyloric spasm soon after birth and again at six months of age. He was breast-fed at first and sucked the two middle fingers of his right hand until the age of five. He did, however, cry frequently and often displayed anger.

Chris seems to have been a happy child. He went off to kindergarten quite willingly and loved school from the start. His younger brother was born when he was six, and he never showed any jealousy of the new baby.

By the age of 8, Chris was crying less and showing less anger and by 12 his emotional outbursts were even less frequent. He had many friends, was enthusiastic about sports, was doing well in school, and had several collections of butterflies and stamps. His mother noted that in seventh grade he was becoming a conformist and was very sensitive. She gives an example of him coming home from school at lunchtime to "talk away" the hurts of the morning.

In most respects, Chris's childhood seems ordinary. But there are some hints that his mother was somewhat disturbed. Mrs. Jens appears to be obsessed by self-analysis. In her book, she reprinted letters in which she lectures everyone, including her husband (whom she refers to as "Dad") and her mother, on what is wrong with them and how healthy she herself is. It seems possible that she sensitized Chris so that he too, like her, became obsessively concerned with his inner psychological states. Almost all children manage to get through their childhood without having to talk twice a day about the things that upset them. Chris's difficulty in coping with his childhood years was most likely caused by his mother. Mrs. Jens was not necessarily disturbed. She is what we call a schizophrenogenic mother — one who makes her children disturbed.

High School

Chris had no major problems in high school. His grades were good and he was popular. He worked in a drugstore for extra money. However, from his letters to friends that are reprinted in the book, we see the beginning of this obsessive self-analysis. For example, to one girlfriend he talked about the problems he was having with his effort to stop smoking; he tried to stop, but when he became depressed or bored he would start again. Then, in disgust he quit once more and this caused him to wonder whether he was a phoney.

He had begun to rebel in junior high school, and in the summer of 1961 he hitchhiked to California from his home in Illinois. His parents worried, but felt that it was best to let him go. His mother mentions a few of Chris's "problems": that his only brush with the law occurred because he had sold alcohol to minors (when he was a minor himself); that he had checked to make sure that his piece of dessert was larger than anyone else's, and that he talked with his mother about his low opinion of himself. It worried him when others liked him; he hated being seen as good or perfect because he was so aware of his faults. He was also embarrassed because he perspired a great deal under the arms.

College

In 1962, Chris went off Cornell University. He soon became involved with a very shy girl named Betty. His mother thought that they were too dependent on each other. Imitating his mother, Chris adopted the role of "helping" Betty with her problems. His grades were fine, but he was rejected by the only fraternity he tried for. He was somewhat nonconformist, and looked the part with his long hair and beard.

During his first summer vacation, Betty went out with another man, and this devastated Chris. His sophomore year began with pain and loneliness. To reassure him Mrs. Jens wrote a letter to her son in which she said that she wished that she had run into someone like him when she was in school, saying that she would have looked past his weaknesses. Mrs. Jens says she is aware that Chris may possibly have had incestuous feelings for her, and she seems to have had similar feelings for her son. It is interesting that she cannot resist emphasizing that Chris has weaknesses. (She says in the same letter that Chris is neurotically in need of a girl. She also sent him a copy of a letter written to a friend by the author James Agee in which he promises not to kill himself.)

During his sophomore year, Chris was still smoking and still trying to quit. He also had a car accident. He broke his fist in a fight with a fellow student and so apparently still had outbursts that were difficult to control. He became interested in the possibility of psychotherapy but there is no indication that he visited a therapist. Mrs. Jens writes that she worried that he might kill himself by throwing himself into the gorge on the Cornell campus. Chris became enamored of Freudian ideas and began to argue a lot with his mother over their different psychological beliefs. Things became increasingly difficult between mother and son. He began to criticize her for everything, even her cooking, refused to kiss her anymore and switched his admiration to his father. During the summer his father bought Chris a motorcycle. This angered Mrs. Jens, and she claims that her husband had an infantile desire to ride a motorcycle himself and that this was his likely motive for buying the bike.

In his junior year, Chris began to get very interested in his psychology courses. He was influenced by Hobart Mowrer and the behaviorists. Chris classified himself as a cycloid personality, with highs and lows. At this time he saw himself as having a manic personality as opposed to the manic-depressive "diagnosis" he gave himself in his sophomore year. In 1965 he became attached to a girl, Karen, whom he regarded as being his superior, so that his relationship with her made him feel inferior. It is interesting to note that Chris appears to have only two roles with women, that of "therapist" or that of "patient," roles that he probably learned from his mother.

In his journal, Chris talks about his anxiety, his anger over his anxiety, his fear of rejection, and his need to impress people. He also discusses his excessive perspiration. He decided to resolve the problem of his need to impress people by getting rid of the conflicting images he tried to project and settling on one consistent image to use in public. It apparently did not occur to him to be himself.

Chris's grandfather died in the spring of 1965, and his relationship with Karen ended. It is possible that Karen grew tired of Chris's continual self-absorption and of being his "guru." Chris took the examination for medical school and established a rigorous schedule involving classes, guitar and Russian study, and work. This left only six hours for him to sleep. He reported periods of apathy (rather than depression).

During the third summer vacation, he worked on a Cornell University project in Nova Scotia. While he was there, he got involved with a girl named Margie. In his senior year, Chris switched his major to ecology. He started to have fights with his father about financial support. His father continued to pay his expenses but, because of the friction, requested that Chris stay away from home.

Margie became pregnant with Chris's child but had an abortion, and the two did not get married. Chris graduated in June 1966 and spent the summer at home making furniture for the family before going off to graduate school to study ecology at the University of Texas. He was still being supported to some extent by his father.

Graduate School and Breakdown

By the time Christmas arrived, Chris began to dislike his professors. He was depressed. In January 1967, he visited the university counseling center but seemed not to find what he wanted there. He and Margie broke up, and soon thereafter she married someone else. Chris began reading about Scientology.

At the beginning of his second year of graduate school, Chris came home unexpectedly. His mother reports that he was difficult to live with and that he argued with his parents about everything. He went back to Texas, but abruptly dropped out of school in November. Over the telephone, he told his mother that he had been "reborn" and that it wasn't necessary to work because the Lord would "provide." He wanted to go home but was afraid to ride in airplanes because he thought that there were evil messages in the noise. He was also afraid to use the telephone. He therefore decided to walk home from Austin. He walked as far as Dallas, but presumably realizing the absurdity of his endeavor, he decided to fly the rest of the way. At home, he immediately began fighting with his parents. He even demanded that his father kick him out of the house. He seemed to be obsessed by the devil and confessed to being very depressed.

As an illustration of his psychotic behavior, Chris went out one evening with a girl he had met, a former psychiatric patient. He stayed up all night with her and in the morning told his mother that great things had happened and that he now had no need to kill his mother or himself in order to "get free." He became excited and made aggressive and sexual remarks to his mother. His parents decided for the first time to hospitalize Chris in January 1968.

Chris made two attempts at suicide in the hospital, trying to push a broken billiard cue into his brain and jumping headfirst into a bathtub. He was hostile toward his family, had periods of catatonia, and sometimes believed he was Christ.

He was released after four months, but he was still hostile and remote. He tried to stab himself in the abdomen with a penknife. One night the police picked him up. While in the cell he yelled for someone to kill him and this prompted a second hospitalization.

After another three months in the hospital, he decided to go back to Austin. He rented a room and got a dishwashing job. He spent most of his money buying mystical and occult books and spent a lot of time reading them. After four months Chris broke down again and was hospitalized in Austin. He was given electroconvulsive therapy, which brought him out of his depression, became manic and then settled down in his "religious" frame of mind. Following his release in the summer, Chris's employer refused to rehire him, so his parents had to support him. He spent his time reading mystical and religious books, attending services, and playing the organ for a Greek Orthodox church.

In April 1970, Chris arrived home without warning. He seemed to need his family, but he was still very hostile toward them. He was thin from fasting and seemed very unstable. His parents hospitalized him the next day. In the hospital he asked his mother, "Dad would be relieved, wouldn't he, if I chose suicide as my answer?" And later, he put his arms around both parents and said, "I can never be happy until you and Dad get together."

After two months, Chris came home unexpectedly and one day early. He was restless and agitated. He ran to a nearby field, poured gasoline on himself and set it alight. His mother put out the flames by beating him with clumps of grass, but he died two days later.

DISCUSSION

Chris was diagnosed as schizophrenic and as schizoaffective, and he was clearly psychotic. It would seem that there was little evidence of psychological disturbance in his early years, though understandably his mother may not be the best source of this information. Apparently, his psychosis came on suddenly while he was in graduate school, with no apparent precipitating cause.

Chris's problem with his mother was obvious to both Chris and Mrs. Jens. It appears that Mr. and Mrs. Jens were distant from each other. They did not sleep together, and to Chris this seemed to imply that his mother was all the more available to him, at least in his unconscious mind. This led to an anxiety with which he could not cope. It was clear to him at the end of his life that his own mental health might depend upon his parents having a healthy marriage. That he turned to religion at the end was perhaps a way for him to deal with his unconscious conflicts and his belief that he was a sinner.

Chris seems to have been ill-served by his mother. Her obsession with mental health and psychology led to his morbid self-absorption and the development of the two problematic roles that he assumed: being both the therapist and the patient. However, unhealthy though this may have been, it cannot be the sole reason for his psychosis and suicide.

It is interesting to note that Chris's hostility was a chronic problem in his life, from outbursts as a kid to arguments as an adolescent, sometimes with his father and more often with his mother. It appears that anger and suicidal depression can coexist.

Chris's attempts at suicide and his effective final act had the style of a schizophrenic. Pushing a billiard cue into one's brain and self-immolation are not common methods for suicide, but someone like Chris was less likely to be able to purchase a gun or collect enough of a lethal medication to kill himself.

Psychiatrists speculate that some people "become crazy" to prevent themselves from committing suicide, while others commit suicide because they are afraid of "becoming crazy." Perhaps Chris killed himself because he could not face life as a schizophrenic.

REFERENCES

Apter, A., A. Bleich, R. Plutchik, S. Mendelsohn and S. Tyano. 1988. Suicidal behavior, depression and conduct disorder in hospitalized adolescents. *Journal of the American Academy of Child and Adolescent Psychiatry* 27:696-699.

Asarnow, J.R. and D. Guthrie. 1989. Suicidal behavior, depression and hopelessness in child psychiatric patients. *Journal of Clinical Child Psychology* 18:129-136.

Beck, A.T., A. Weissman, D. Lester and L. Trexler. 1974. The measurement of pessimism. *Journal of Consulting and Clinical Psychology* 42:861-865.

Cole, D.A. 1989. Psychopathology of adolescent suicide. *Journal of Abnormal Psychology* 98:248-255.

Jens, L. 1987. *The Jewelled Flower*. Aurora, CO: National Writers Press.

Temoche, A., T.F. Pugh and B. MacMahon. 1964. Suicide rates among current and former mental institution patients. *Journal of Nervous and Mental Disease* 138:124-130.

Chapter 6

Perinatal Influences on Adolescent Suicide

Eric Berne (1961) proposed a theory of the human mind and a system of psychotherapy (transactional analysis) that he based on Freud's psychoanalytic theory. Among the new ideas proposed by Berne was the concept of a *script* — a system principle describing the organization of a person's mind or his life as a whole. Steiner (1974) saw scripts as conscious life plans made in childhood that influence and make predictable the rest of one's life. Steiner described three basic life scripts: *no love* (the actual state of depression), *no mind* (madness) and *no joy* (addiction). He also described particular manifestations of life scripts that are commonly seen in clients.

Suicide in transactional analysis is seen as deriving from an injunction given to the child typically by the parents (Woollams et al. 1977). Infants need permission to exist and to belong in the world. From the moment of birth infants receive from parents and significant others verbal and nonverbal messages about whether they are really wanted. The infant or child can receive a "don't exist" message at any age and in various ways: perhaps the infant is handled stiffly or with distaste; perhaps a parent actually says "I wish you'd never been born."

These "don't exist" injunctions can come from the

mother's or father's judgmental parenting role ("You are bad! Go away!") and they can also come from the parent's immature side ("I hate you! You are a nuisance!") The father may be jealous of the attention his wife gives to the newborn. The mother may resent having the family pressure of raising children (Stewart and Joines 1987). If several significant others make these "don't exist" injunctions, then the injunction will be stronger than when only one significant other makes the injunction.

This injunction becomes part of the individual's script. Since these injunctions are made to the child, they become part of the immature, possibly unconscious, part of the mind. Thus, in later life, even though the individual's rational conscious mind may make a decision not to commit suicide, the individual's immature and unconscious state must also accept this decision for the individual to be free of suicidal impulses.

Children may also perceive "don't exist" injunctions when they do not actually exist. If a child hears his parents say that his birth was a difficult one, it may cause him to think that just by being born he has hurt his mother. This thought may make the child think, "I am dangerous and therefore I deserve to be hurt or killed."

PRIMAL SCREAM THERAPY

Arthur Janov's (1972) theory of how disturbed behavior develops is in many respects similar to psychoanalytic theory. Janov believed that babies have important psychological and physiological needs that must be gratified. These needs, called *primal needs,* include being fed, kept warm, being held and being stimulated. Some babies have their needs ignored, and others have parents who fail to gratify these needs. Some babies suffer more frustration when their needs are not fulfilled than do other babies. If his needs are consistently frustrated, the baby will learn to block out the emotions that accompany this deprivation and with continued severe deprivation, the baby will also learn to repress the needs themselves, and will pursue substitute gratifications instead. Developing and satisfying substitute needs symbolically satisfies primal needs and this is the essential cause of neurotic behavior.

Janov (1974) felt that certain aspects of the birth process were a source for suicide later in life. He felt that when people turn to suicide as a solution for ending pain, it is the result of a prototypic trauma that usually occurred around the time of birth, when death was perceived as the *only* solution. When the notion of death as the only alternative becomes an unconscious memory it will shape the way the person thinks about solving overwhelming problems later in life. Pain during or soon after birth often involves near-death situations, and if that pain is carried to an extreme, death is often the result. Being left totally alone without warmth or human touch immediately after birth and umbilical strangulation during birth, are examples of such sources of pain.

Traumas occurring in the first few years of life can also set up a death-thought syndrome, but these traumas are usually *possible-death* events. Janov presents the case of a woman who had been raped by her father when she was three years old and who had attempted suicide several times. This catastrophic trauma happened at an age when there seemed to be no other way to end the pain but through death. Later, any stress or hurt reactivated the earlier pain, and the suicidal thoughts would reoccur.

The method chosen for suicide may be related to the primal pain experienced. One suicidal woman slashed her wrists with razor blades because she wanted to see the blood ooze out. In the course of primal scream therapy, she recalled an incident that occurred at the age of six when her father hit her in the face. She had smeared the blood from her nose onto the wall to show her parents how much she hurt. Blood became the symbol for making her hurt known to others. Another patient thought of hanging himself whenever he was upset. During his primal re-encounters he lived through the experience of nearly being strangled at birth.

Suicide is made more likely if, in addition to the primal trauma, there is also a repressive home atmosphere that stifles the outward expression of pain. As a result, the person can only turn inward to experience the pain, and the crushing weight of this inverted pain can eventually lead to suicide.

More recently, Grof (1985) speculated that the choice of suicide method is based upon one's earliest memories, particularly during the birth process. Those who choose nonviolent methods for suicide, especially medications, in order to escape physical and psychological pain, have inhibited depressions and are seeking a return to an intrauterine existence. In contrast, those choosing violent methods for committing suicide have agitated depressions and are seeking to intensify their suffering in order to achieve the same type of liberation that they experienced in the birth process.

Speculative though such views may be, Salk and his team (1985) found that adolescents who committed suicide were more likely to have suffered respiratory distress at birth than were nonsuicidal adolescents. Similarly, Jacobson and his colleagues (1987) found that the choice of method for suicide in adults was associated with birth conditions; those who committed suicide by asphyxiation (hanging, strangulation, drowning or gas) were more likely to have experienced asphyxia at birth. Those who chose violent methods for suicide (hanging, jumping or firearms) had often experienced birth trauma associated with having been on life support equipment.

DISCUSSION

It may be that the speculations and research mentioned above will not necessarily withstand further empirical testing. However, it is interesting to consider the possibility that the seeds for suicide may be sown much earlier in life than we had previously suspected. This idea would certainly further our understanding of suicide.

Freud believed that suicide was caused when a person lost someone with whom he had closely identified as a child, and the anger once directed toward the loved one then becomes redirected inward (Litman 1967). The speculations presented above amplify this formulation by suggesting that this process is more likely to occur when the loved one with whom the child identified harbored hostile wishes toward the child and, in particular, conscious or unconscious desires for the child's nonexistence. Then, not only will the child feel anger toward a lost significant other with whom he identified, but also, by identifying with this hostile loved one, the child will have adopted the other's hostile wishes toward himself. When this is the situation, the child is destined for eventual self-destruction.

REFERENCES

Berne, E. 1961. *Transactional Analysis in Psychotherapy*. New York: Grove Press.

Grof, S. 1985. *Beyond the Brain*. Albany: State University of New York Press.

Janov, A. 1972. *The Primal Scream*. New York: Dell.

Janov, A. 1974. Further implications of "levels of consciousness." *Journal of Primal Therapy* 1(3):193-212.

Jacobson, B., G. Eklund, L. Hamberger, D. Linnarson, G. Sedvall and M. Valverius. 1987. Perinatal origin of adult self-destructive behavior. *Acta Psychiatrica Scandinavica* 76:364-371.

Litman, R. 1976. Sigmund Freud on Suicide. In E. Shneidman, ed., *Essays in Self-destruction*. New York: Science House.

Salk, L., L. Lipsitt, W. Sturner, B. Reilly and R. Levat. 1985. Relationship of maternal and perinatal conditions to eventual adolescent suicide. *Lancet* 1:624-627.

Steiner, C. 1974. *Scripts People Live*. New York: Grove Press.

Stewart, I. and V. Joines. 1974. *TA Today*. Chapel Hill, NC: Lifespace.

Woollams, S., M. Brown and K. Huige. 1977. What transactional analysts want their clients to know. In G. Barnes, ed., *Transactional Analysis After Eric Berne*. New York: Harper's College Press.

Chapter 7

Childhood Experiences and Adolescent Suicide

A number of studies have explored the association between specific childhood experiences and later suicidal behavior. While most of these studies have focused on one or two particular childhood experiences, such as the loss of a parent to death or divorce, other studies have explored a variety of childhood experiences.

Cynthia Pfeffer and her colleagues carefully studied a group of children from one community. They found that suicidality in these children was moderately associated with assaultiveness, anger, and aggression (Pfeffer et al. 1983). Some of the children were suicidal, and they were more likely to have a depressive disorder; others were only assaultive and they tended to have developmental disorders; still others were both suicidal and assaultive and these children were more likely to have a borderline personality disorder. The suicidal children were more likely to have suicidal parents, while the assaultive children were more likely to have assaultive parents.

They also found that the suicidal children had had more recent and past depressive episodes, they showed more recent aggression, and their parents had had more separations, depressive episodes and psychiatric hospitalizations (Pfeffer et al. 1984) than nonsuicidal children from the same community.

In a study of adolescents who were current psychiatric patients, Pfeffer found that suicidal adolescents were more depressed than the nonsuicidal psychiatric patients. They also showed more recent aggression, abused alcohol more often, more frequently had suicidal mothers, had been physically and sexually abused and were more often diagnosed as having either a major depressive disorder, an adjustment disorder or a developmental disorder. They were less often diagnosed as having mental retardation or schizophrenia, and had a greater preoccupation with death than nonsuicidal psychiatric patients (Pfeffer et al. 1988-89).

Suicidal adolescents, therefore, often seem to come from dysfunctional families and to have suffered more trauma in their early years than adolescents who are not suicidal. They are likely to be severely depressed and to have depressed parents. They also seem to have behavioral problems and are more likely to be angry and assaultive than nonsuicidal adolescents.

PHYSICAL AND SEXUAL ABUSE

A number of studies have appeared in recent years that have documented a high incidence of physical and sexual abuse during the childhoods of suicidal adolescents. For example, Plummer and co-workers (1989) found that adolescent suicide attempters had experienced more physical and sexual abuse than adolescents who only had suicidal thoughts and those who were altogether not suicidal. Similarly, Smith and Crawford (1986) found that high school students who had attempted suicide had experienced more physical beatings, rapes and sexual abuse than other students.

Children who are, or have been, physically and sexually abused are also more likely to be psychiatrically disturbed. Plummer's adolescent suicide attempters were also more often diagnosed as having major depressive disorders, and

Smith and Crawford's adolescent attempters were more depressed. It may be that physical and sexual abuse leads to a greater likelihood of suicide because it increases the chances of becoming psychiatrically disturbed in general and depressed in particular.

It is common for runaway children to have a history of abuse and, as might be expected, runaway children have a high incidence of suicidal preoccupation. For example, Nilson (1981) compared runaways with other children referred from county agencies and found more abuse and more suicide attempts in the backgrounds of the runaways. There have been many other studies that have reported the association between experience of physical and sexual abuse and adolescent suicidal preoccupation, but there have also been studies that report no association (for example, Spirito et al. 1987). There have been no studies published that have reported *less* suicidal preoccupation in those who have been abused.

CHILDHOOD LOSS

It is commonly reported that a child's experience of the loss of one or both parents (through death or divorce) is associated with later-life depression and suicidal thoughts. Lester (1989) has suggested that the losses that occur to those between the ages of 6 and 14 may be especially responsible for causing later suicidal behavior. After investigating the lives of 30 famous adult suicides, Lester found that 16 of them had experienced some kind of loss during the ages of 6 to 14. Most of these suicides had lost their father through death.

Bagley (1989) found that adolescent completed suicides had been in foster or adoptive care and had been separated from their biological parents more often than other adolescents, and research on adolescent suicide attempters has frequently reported similar parental loss (Garfinkel et al. 1982; Grossi 1987). Lester and Beck (1976) argued that early loss is likely to lead to suicidal behavior especially when the person faces additional losses later in life; these later losses re-arouse the pain experienced during the earlier loss, thereby exacerbating the current pain.

In a review of the research on adolescents and adults, Schaller and Schmidtke (1988) estimated that there was a 40 percent incidence of broken homes in completed suicides and a 47 percent incidence in attempted suicides. The incidence of broken homes was also high in drug abusers (43 percent) and juvenile delinquents (44 percent), lower in general psychiatric patients (24 percent), alcoholics (28 percent) and in the "average" person (17 percent).

SCHOOL PERFORMANCE

Studies consistently show that suicidal adolescents do not perform as well in school as nonsuicidal adolescents. Their grade point averages are lower (Reynolds 1988), and they are more often absent from school, more often drop-out and have more discipline problems (Pronovost 1987). Harter and Marold (1987) found that middle-school children (sixth, seventh and eighth graders) who were suicidal were more likely to feel that their achievements were far below what their parents expected from them.

PERSONALITY TRAITS OF SUICIDAL ADOLESCENTS

Although a large number of personality traits have been explored for their potential association with suicidal preoccupation in adolescents, the findings often conflict. Results consistently indicate that suicidal adolescents are more often emotionally disturbed (Simons and Murphy 1985) and have lower self-esteem (Bagley 1975) than nonsuicidal adolescents. In one study, scores on a measure of self-esteem were used to *predict* whether seventh graders would attempt suicide in the following year (Kaplan 1978).

There is the possibility that suicidal adolescents may also

blame others for their misfortunes and unhappiness (rather than blaming themselves) and that they are not as good at finding solutions to the problems they face, but the results of the research in this area are not completely consistent (Lester 1992).

In keeping with Pfeffer's research findings mentioned earlier in this chapter, suicidal adolescents are sometimes found to be more aggressive, more delinquent and more impulsive (Kashani et al. 1989) than nonsuicidal children (Cairns et al. 1988), and this is true of both completed and attempted suicides (Husain and Vandiver 1984) and those with only suicidal thoughts (Kashani et al. 1989).

ADOLESCENTS AND THEIR PARENTS

The families of suicidal adolescents tend to be more chaotic than the families of normal adolescents. Their parents, for example, move, divorce and remarry more (Jacobs 1971).

Grossi (1987) found that the adolescents in a residential treatment program who had previously attempted suicide more often had parents who had problematic marriages, difficulty with their jobs and with parenting. He also reports that adolescent suicide attempters more often felt that no one cared about them.

The parents of suicidal adolescents also more often tend to be psychiatrically disturbed than the parents of normal adolescents. Kashani and his collaborators (1989) found that adolescents with current suicidal ideation had parents with greater psychopathology than did nonsuicidal adolescents. Kerfoot (1988) found the adolescent suicide attempters had more family members with psychiatric disturbances (especially their mothers). Adolescent attempters also more often had suicidal preoccupations and more often committed crimes.

The parents and other family members of suicidal adolescents are more suicidal themselves. Farberow and his team (1987) found that youths with suicidal ideation in one community were more likely to have had friends and family members who had committed suicide than were nonsuicidal youths. Fritz (1987) found that college students who had thought of suicide were more likely to have had family members who had attempted or completed suicide. Garfinkel and co-workers (1982) found that the adolescent suicide attempters (and, among the attempters, the more serious ones) in one emergency room were more likely to have a family history of attempted and completed suicide than the other patients in the emergency room.

Suicidal adolescents also have poor relationships with their parents. For example, Wright (1985) found that high school students and college students who had recent suicidal ideation had worse relationships with their fathers, their parents were more often in conflict and were depressed or angry, their fathers more often abused alcohol and they suffered more physical abuse from their parents.

FAMILY PATTERNS

Some studies have looked at the patterns of interaction in those families where there was a suicidal adolescent. Williams and Lyons (1976) found that these families showed more conflict when discussing a problem, had less effective methods of communication, made fewer positive statements to one another and achieved less final consensus than families with nonsuicidal adolescents. Abraham (1978) found that in families with a suicidal adolescent there was less spontaneous agreement and they described themselves as less effective than did other families.

DISCUSSION

The discussed research indicates that suicidal adolescents tend to have experienced some sort of physical or sexual abuse and the loss of parents during childhood, and to have disturbed family relationships. Their family life tends to be chaotic and their parents are also often disturbed and suicidal themselves. Suicidal adolescents are often emotionally disturbed and have low self-esteem.

These characteristics are also found more often in the backgrounds of suicidal adults, but the presence of these factors has not been explored in the backgrounds of elderly suicides. It may turn out that these factors are less salient for the suicidal behavior of the elderly, but we do not know this for sure yet.

As noted earlier, the impact of these negative childhood experiences on suicide may not be direct. Rather, these experiences may increase the risk of psychiatric disturbance, especially depressive disorders, and it may be the psychiatric disorder that is the precipitating agent that increases the risk of suicide. There have been no studies to explore this possibility, but hopefully new research will help us learn more about this.

REFERENCES

Abraham, Y. 1978. Patterns of communication versus rejection in families of suicidal adolescents. *Dissertation Abstracts International* 38A:4669.

Bagley, C. 1975. Suicidal behavior and suicidal ideation in adolescents. *British Journal of Guidance and Counseling* 3:190-208.

Bagley, C. 1989. Profiles of youthful suicide. *Psychological Reports* 65:234.

Cairns, R.B., G. Peterson and H.J. Neckerman. 1988. Suicidal behavior in aggressive adolescents. *Journal of Clinical Child Psychology* 17:2998-3309.

Farberow, N.L., R.E. Litman and F.L. Nelson. 1987. A survey of youth suicide in California. In R. Yufit, ed., *Proceedings of the 20th Annual Conference*. Denver: American Association of Suicidology.

Fritz, D. 1987. Suicide ideation. In R. Yufit, ed., *Proceedings of the 20th Annual Conference*. Denver: American Association of Suicidology.

Garfinkel, B.D., A. Froese and J. Hood. 1982. Suicide attempts in children and adolescents. *American Journal of Psychiatry*. 139:1257-1261.

Grossi, V. 1987. Deliberate self-harm among adolescents in residential treatment centers. In R. Yufit, ed., *Proceedings of the 20th Annual Conference*. Denver: American Association of Suicidology.

Harter, S. and D. Marold. 1987. Familial values and adolescent suicidal ideation. In R. Yufit, ed., *Proceedings of the 20th Annual Conference*. Denver: American Association of Suicidology.

Husain, S.A. and T. Vandiver. 1984. *Suicide in Children and Adolescents*. New York: Spectrum Books.

Jacobs, J. 1971. *Adolescent Suicide*. New York: Wiley.

Kaplan, H.B. 1978. Self-attitudes and multiple modes of deviance. In D. Lettieri, ed., *Drugs and Suicide*. Beverly Hills, CA: Sage.

Kashani, J. H., P. Goddard, P and J.C. Reid. 1989. Correlates of suicidal ideation in a community sample of children and adolescents. *Journal of the American Academy of Child and Adolescent Psychiatry* 28:912-917.

Kerfoot, M. 1988. Deliberate self-poisoning in childhood and early adolescence. *Journal of Child Psychology and Psychiatry*. 29:335-343.

Lester, D. 1989. Experience of parental loss and later suicide. *Acta Psychiatrica Scandinavica* 79:450-452.

Lester, D. 1992. *Why People Kill Themselves*. Springfield, IL: Charles C. Thomas.

Lester, D., and A.T. Beck. 1976. Early loss as a possible sensitizer to later loss in attempted suicides. *Psychological Reports* 39:121-122.

Nilson, P. 1981. Psychological profiles of runaway children and adolescents. In C.F. Wells and I.R. Stuart, eds., *Self-Destructive Behavior in Children and Adolescents.* New York: Van Nostrand Reinhold.

Pfeffer, C., D. Adams, A. Weiner, A. and J. Rosenberg. 1988. Life event stresses on parents on suicidal children. *International Journal of Family Psychiatry* 9:341-350.

Pfeffer, C., J. Newcorn, G. Kaplan, M. Mizruchi and R. Plutchik. 1989. Subtypes of suicidal and assaultive behaviors in adolescent psychiatric inpatients. *Journal of Child Psychology and Psychiatry* 30:151-163.

Pfeffer, C., R. Plutchik and M. Mizruchi 1983. Suicide and assaultive behavior in children. *American Journal of Psychiatry* 140:154-157.

Pfeffer, C., S. Zuckerman, P. Plutchik and M. Mizruchi. 1984. Suicidal behavior in normal school children. *Journal of the American Academy of Child Psychiatry* 23:416-423.

Plummer, B., M. Gispert, R. Hayden, D. Robbins, D. and R. Seifer. R. 1989. Depression, hopelessness, and substance abuse among hospitalized adolescents with suicidal ideation or behavior. Paper presented at the International Association for Suicide Prevention, Brussels.

Pronovost, Y. 1987. Adaptive profile of adolescents with suicidal tendencies in the Quebec school system. In R. Yufit, ed., *Proceedings of the 20th Annual Conference.* Denver: American Association of Suicidology.

Reynolds, W. M. 1988. *Suicidal Ideation Questionnaire.* Odessa, FL: Psychological Assessment Resources.

Schaller, S. and A. Schmidtke. 1988. Broken homes and suicidal behavior. In H.J. Moller, A. Schmidtke, and R. Welz, eds., *Current Issues of Suicidology.* Berlin: Springer-Verlag.

Simons, R.L. and P.I. Murphy. 1985. Sex differences in the causes of adolescent suicide ideation. *Journal of Youth and Adolescence* 14:423-434.

Smith, K. and S. Crawford. 1986. Suicidal behavior among normal high school students. *Suicide and Life-Threatening Behavior* 16:313-325.

Spirito, A. L. Stark, M. Fristad, K. Hart, K. and J.Owens-Stively. 1987. Adolescent suicide attempters on a pediatric unit. *Journal of Pediatric Psychology* 12:171-189.

Williams, C. and C.M. Lyons. 1976. Family interaction and adolescent suicidal behavior. *Australian and New Zealand Journal of Psychiatry* 10:243-252.

Wright, L. 1985. Suicidal thoughts and their relationship to family stress and personal problems among high school seniors and college undergraduates. *Adolescence* 20:575-580.

Chapter 8

Suicide Clusters and Subcultures

example

One may occasionally hear about stories of *clusters* of suicides. This refers to a situation in which *several* people kill themselves (or try to) as a result of another suicide. Often, people in the community become anxious that these grouped suicides will continue; however, these types of suicidal acts usually become less frequent over a short period of time. Coleman (1987) has documented many of these clusters.

Because the media tends to focus mainly on clusters of teenage suicide many believe that clustering does not occur with adults, but this is not the case. Clustered suicides, especially in institutions, happen among adults with equal frequency. For example, Lester and Danto (1992) reported a cluster of suicides among inmates in one prison, and Kirch and Lester (1986) found evidence for a clustering of suicides in a small town in England by adults who used plastic bags to suffocate themselves.

Clustering is also found for nonlethal suicidal behavior. For example, Hankoff (1979) reported a cluster of suicide attempts in an overseas United States Marine base that was apparently stimulated by the suicide attempt of a marine who was dismissed from his post as a consequence of this action.

Self-mutilation, such as delicate wrist-cutting, also shows evidence of clustering and contagion, especially among adolescent psychiatric inpatients, where wrist-cutting by one patient is followed by a copy-cat wrist-cutting by several others on the ward.

There is a great deal of evidence that the suicide of a celebrity is followed in the next few days by an increase in the number of suicides (Stack 1990). Stack found that suicides by people such as Marilyn Monroe and Freddie Prinze generated, on average, an extra 220 suicides during the month of publicity. (While it is now debatable whether Marilyn Monroe did in fact kill herself, the message given by the media at the time of her death was that it *was* a suicide.) The suicides of political figures can also cause a copy-cat effect; when Secretary of Defense James Forrestal committed suicide, it triggered about 50 additional suicides. There is some evidence also that suicides by characters in television shows, such as soap operas and even in programs designed to sensitize viewers to the problems of suicide, can trigger suicides in the days following broadcast. Stack found that this phenomenon occurred in adolescents, young adults and in the elderly, but not in middle-aged adults. Stack speculated that perhaps middle age is not a period marked by a high risk of suicide and maybe this is the reason that most middle-aged people do not respond to publicity about suicide.

Consider this example of clusters of suicide in young adults: Yukiko Okada, an 18-year-old singing idol in Japan, was unhappy about her love affair with an actor. She was found on April 8, 1986, at 10 a.m., in a gas-filled apartment in Tokyo, alive, but with her wrists slashed. She was revived and treated, but two hours later she climbed to the roof of a seven-story recording studio and jumped to her death. The place where she landed on the street became a shrine. People placed wreaths there and, within a day of her death, others began to copy her suicide. Thirty-three young people took their lives in the 17 days following her death, many of them jumping to their death as she did. One month after this incident, 21-year-old Masanno Majima jumped from the same roof as Yukiko and landed on her shrine. He had a photograph of Yukiko in his pocket — an indication that he surely had her in mind when he killed himself.

As discussed elsewhere in this book, research indicates that the suicides of young people are more often a response to interpersonal frictions with friends and lovers or problems with parents when compared to the suicides of older adults which are more often due to long-standing personal problems such as depression, psychiatric illness and substance abuse. Perhaps adolescents are more sensitive to events in their cultural milieu, and so these suicidal stimuli from celebrities have a more powerful effect on them.

Most of the publicized cases of clusters of teenage suicides are reported superficially in the news, and in-depth analysis of the teenagers involved is rarely included. However, one cluster of three teenagers from a close-knit group of five has been described in some detail below by Fried (1984).

A CASE HISTORY OF A CLUSTER OF TEENAGE SUICIDES

In this group of five friends, Marc (aged 17) and Dan (aged 16), while high on LSD, handcuffed themselves together and jumped to their death into a quarry. Just over two months later, Michelle (aged 16), who had been Marc's girlfriend, shot herself in the chest. These three suicides triggered a great deal of suicidal behavior in other teenagers at their high school (suicide attempts, threats of suicide and suicidal preoccupation), but no other students killed themselves.

The Leader

The leader of this particular group was Marc, the oldest. He began dating Michelle. At that time, Michelle's friend Caitlin joined the group, as did Marc's friends Dan and Jim. Eventually, Caitlin began to date Dan.

Drug Involvement

The three boys were using drugs extensively. Their preferred drug was LSD, but they also used speed and alcohol. The girls disapproved of drug use and tried LSD only once. Because the girls disapproved of their drug use, the boys began to use drugs only when the girls were absent so they wouldn't know about the extent of their use.

Music

The music that the group liked to listen to was heavy metal, and Marc and Dan especially were very involved in this kind of music. Marc used to draw in the pictorial style that accompanies this music — rocket ships, crashing cars, muscular hulks fighting with flaming torches, and rock guitarists in crazed, contorted positions. Dan played "air guitar" while he was in school and daydreamed of being a musician.

Many people have blamed heavy metal music for the behavioral problems of teenagers. The lyrics are full of of gory apocalypse and religious allusions, violence and nihilism. Rap music is also criticized for having a similarly negative influence on its listeners.

In my opinion, this is a rather simplistic view. Teenagers have particular values and attitudes and it is very likely that they will be drawn to music and media presentations that appeal to these attitudes. Heavy metal music facilitates the arousal of particular desires and emotions, and perhaps other music served a similar purpose in earlier times.

Relationships with Parents

Marc was extremely alienated from his parents. His father was a Lutheran minister, and Marc refused to have any involvement in religion. He fought with his parents and verbally abused his mother. A few months prior to his death, he left home to live with Jim's parents. Marc's parents portrayed themselves to Fried, the journalist who investigated this story, as caring and concerned parents, but perhaps Fried was not aware of, or sensitive to, possible interpersonal problems in this dysfunctional family. In fact, there are signs that Marc's parents were authoritarian and indifferent despite their veneer of concern. For example, when Marc walked out after a fight with them one day, he was so upset that he verbally threatened to commit suicide. Despite this serious threat both parents ignored him and chose to leave to fulfill a previous commitment his father had made to preside at a funeral. Dan, too, was alienated from his parents, but they did not fight very much because Dan kept most of his life hidden from them. While Dan's parents refused to talk to Fried, and we therefore do not have direct information from them, they seemed to be completely in the dark regarding what was going on in their son's life, and after his death, they refused to accept the fact that he had killed himself. In a tape recording the boys made just before they jumped to their deaths, Marc expressed hatred for his parents, whereas Dan seemed indifferent to his parents.

Michelle, who was referred to a counselor after the boys killed themselves, also appeared have problems with her parents. The counselor felt that she was full of rage and was intensely resentful toward her parents. Caitlin and Jim, on the other hand, seemed to have more normal relationships with their parents.

Self-Image

Marc had a very poor self-image. Although talented, he saw himself as a loser and as someone who did not deserve anything good. For example, he refused birthday and Christmas presents because he felt that he did not deserve them. His family had a history of early death; few of the males had ever lived past 35 years of age. His father had reached the age of 45, but recently underwent triple bypass surgery. He suffered a heart attack after the operation and survived, but he was still very sick.

Both Michelle and Caitlin had poor self-images. Michelle was shy, small and asthmatic. She felt that she was not attractive and in particular hated her nose. She was ill at ease in groups and preferred to have one friend at a time, someone with whom she could spend all her time. Her parents were very rich, and she hated the ostentation of the money, but did not want to lose the benefits of it. Girls from her school called her a "rich bitch."

Caitlin also disliked the way she looked. She was an Army brat whose father was continually moving around the world and was often away on assignment. In fact, he was absent during much of this crisis.

Loss

At the time Marc killed himself, he and Michelle were still dating. Caitlin had broken up with Dan because of his increasing drug use and moodiness and their continual fighting. She began to see more of Jim. Dan was primarily focusing on his loss of Caitlin when he talked on the tape he had made prior to his death.

As a result of his suicide, Michelle lost her boyfriend Marc. Together with Caitlin and Jim, she had been the first to find the bodies of Marc and Dan at the quarry. She talked of wanting to be with Marc. She began to copy his mannerisms, and she decorated her room with his clothes, posters and records. When she shot herself, a photograph of Marc was on the car seat next to her.

Suicidal Preoccupation

Along with Marc's preoccupation over his anticipated early death, he made a suicide attempt by trying to jump into the quarry in front of the rest of the group. Michelle took an overdose of pills at home about six weeks before her death. However, Michelle denied any suicidal intent to Caitlin before taking her life. Dan made many suicidal threats before his death, and his girlfriend Caitlin began consulting Marc about Dan's state. People at school, including a counselor and several students, knew that Marc and Dan had suicidal intentions, and they even knew they had bought 22 hits of LSD that day. Even though all of these people were aware of this, they all wanted to believe that things were fine.

DISCUSSION

The concept of subcultures has become very popular in theories of behavior in recent years. A subculture is a culture that exists within a larger culture. A subculture has its own customs, values and attitudes and shapes behaviors by rewarding some actions and punishing others. This brief description of a cluster of teenage suicides has suggested several elements of the teenage suicidal subculture. There was drug involvement, relationships with parents that were either full of resentment or indifference. They all had poor self-images, including components of unworthiness and feelings of ugliness, with symptoms of shyness and dependency on others or on a small number of peers. There was also the probable loss of a lover (though Fried does not report on the sexual relations between members of the group). There was great involvement with fantasies stimulated by heavy metal music and daydreams of being musicians.

Although this particular group was quite self-contained, their suicides generated a great deal of suicidal preoccupation and acting-out by other students in their school. This suggests that the subcultural values the group had were quite widespread. Interestingly, feelings of hostility were also aroused. One girl overdosed on Tylenol and, on her return to school, found a full bottle of Tylenol in her locker with a note saying, "Do it right next time." After Marc's suicide, someone wrote on Michelle's locker, "You killed him."

These five teenagers clearly formed a peer group. However, the fact that their behaviors tapped into a suicidal vein among the other students in the high school points to the existence of a peer subculture that transcended the peer group. Competition for status frequently occurs within each peer group, and this leads to experimentation with new behaviors. Thus, behaviors within a peer group, and therefore the peer subculture, tend to become more extreme. In a suicidal subculture, overt suicidal acts seem inevitable given time. The existence of large numbers of peer groups in the peer subculture and the experimentation by peer groups with new behaviors mean that the subculture is dynamic over time, and is continually modified. Therefore, the teenage suicidal subculture in the next few years may be significantly different from the present subculture.

The concept of subculture is useful since it focuses our awareness on what values and attitudes accompany participation in a particular life style. It draws our attention to the social shaping of behavior that can take place and leads us to ask what facilitates the entry of people into the subculture and maintains their presence in the subculture once there.

Adolescents seem to be especially sensitive to the suicidal behavior of others. Their decision to kill themselves or to attempt suicide can on occasion be affected by suicidal behavior in their friends, family members and aquaintances and by suicidal behavior in celebrities. This makes their suicidal actions sometimes surprising since we do not typically expect life and death decisions to be made impulsively and in imitation of others.

REFERENCES

Coleman, L. 1987. *Suicide Clusters*. Boston: Faber & Faber.

Fried, S. 1984. Over the edge. *Philadelphia Magazine*, October, 1-17.

Hankoff, L. 1979. The armed forces. In L. Hankoff and B. Einsidler, eds., *Suicide*. Littleton, MA: PSG Publishers.

Kirch, M.R. and D. Lester. 1986. Clusters of suicide. *Psychological Reports* 59:1126.

Lester, D. 1987. *Suicide as a Learned Behavior*. Springfield, IL: Charles C Thomas.

Lester, D. and B. Danto. *1993. Suicide Behind Bars*. Philadelphia: The Charles Press.

Stack, S. 1990. Media impacts on suicide. In D. Lester, ed., *Current Concepts of Suicide*. Philadelphia: The Charles Press.

Chapter 9

Double Suicides and Suicide Pacts

Although there are some famous double suicide pacts, such as that of Romeo and Juliet in Shakespeare's play, double suicides and suicide pacts are actually quite rare and mostly involve the elderly. However, suicide pacts among adolescents do occur.

In Dade County, Florida, Fishbain and Aldrich (1985) found that 0.007 percent of suicides involved suicide pacts. The majority of those who made the pacts were married and unemployed and had experienced recent loss or financial problems.

Rosenbaum (1983) reviewed six cases of suicide pacts in which one of the participants survived. The instigator of the suicide pact was typically male, psychiatrically depressed and had a history of attempted suicide and ultimately succeeded in killing himself. The survivor was usually female and was neither psychiatrically disturbed nor had a history of attempted suicide. Wickett (1989) documented 97 cases of double suicides involving spouses in the United States in the 1980s. Two-thirds of these were mercy killings followed by the suicide of the other, and one-third were double suicides. In the typical case, the wife or both partners were suffering. The husband was usually the instigator because he could not bear his wife's suffering or the prospect of life without her. The couple felt exhausted and helpless by their problems and had a fear of being apart from each other or being institutionalized. In the double suicides, the decision was more mutual and less impulsive, and there was less despondency.

Suicide pacts and double suicides clearly are not common events and very little research has appeared on them. Nevertheless, suicide pacts do occur, and sometimes they occur in adolescents. One particular suicide pact in 1969 involving two high school students intrigued Eliot Asinof, and he wrote a book on it (Asinof 1971). Their story follows.

CRAIG AND JOAN

Craig Badialis was 17 years old when he and his girlfriend, Joan Fox, killed themselves. They committed suicide on the evening of a Peace Moratorium rally at Glassboro State College in New Jersey on October 16, 1969. Between the two of them, Craig and Joan left 24 suicide notes. While most of their notes were supressed by the police, those that were made available said that they had killed themselves as a sacrifice to motivate people to do something peaceful and constructive with their lives.

Craig and Joan were long-time sweethearts. They were both good but not brilliant students and were popular. Craig was head of the high school dramatic society and Joan was a cheerleader. They had no history of unorthodox behavior. In fact, they were both apparently well-adjusted and clean-cut.

Craig's Family

Craig had one brother, Bernie, who was four years his senior. Their father, Bernard, was 50 years old and worked as the foreman of a carpenter's crew in Philadelphia. His father had emigrated from Italy in the 1920s. Bernard had grown up during the Depression, served in the Second World War and then in the Air Force for 22 years before retiring. He met his wife Dolly in New Jersey after the war while home on leave. Dolly's father was also a skilled worker, and his four sons all became tradesmen and union members in Philadelphia. Bernard and Dolly had three children, but their first baby died shortly after birth.

Because of their father's tours cf duty, the boys grew up without seeing much of their father. Mr. Badialis retirement was hard for his sons who now had to deal with a traditional military-trained father. He was hard on them, especially Craig, and Bernie was clearly his favorite. At 17, Bernie was tall, lean and athletic and he was on the high school football and baseball teams. Thirteen-year-old Craig was fat and clumsy compared to his brother.

Mr. Badialis went bowling once a week with the church league, spent some evenings at the Freemason's Lodge, and also spent time hunting. Bernie hunted with his father, but Craig disliked killing. Bernard was Catholic and Dolly was Methodist, and they brought up their children Episcopalian. The family went to church every Sunday morning, and Bernard served in the vestry.

Bernie had spent two years at Brevard College in North Carolina. He then moved back to his parent's house with his wife, Margaret, and their baby. They moved into Craig's room, and Craig had to move into the basement. Bernie began attending courses at Glassboro State College with the goal of becoming a teacher.

Craig's Early Years

Craig was born in Blackwood, New Jersey. His family moved to Hawaii for one year, but soon Mrs. Badialis went back home to Blackwood and waited for her husband's return. As a baby, Craig seldom slept well. He cried throughout the night, but the doctor said that Craig was not colicky or sick, just overactive.

Craig had some musical talent and played piano, saxophone and also the guitar. His grades were average, but his teachers saw him as lazy and unmotivated. His mother was kind and lenient and tried to soften her husband's strict discipline. Bernie recalled that there was a lot of hostility between the father and the two sons, with Craig suffering at the hands of both his father and his older brother.

Craig at High School

When Craig was 14, his brother Bernie went to college. Free from the competition with Bernie, Craig developed his own style. He liked girls and became friendly with several of them. In 9th grade, he discovered Joan and dramatics. Acting in and producing plays for the school became a central hobby for Craig. He also began to write stories, poems, and long letters.

He continued to play the guitar and liked the music of Janis Ian, Leonard Cohen, Joni Mitchell and Peter, Paul and Mary. Although his son's interest did not especially please his father, Bernard did not discourage Craig and even bought him a 12-string guitar for his 16th birthday.

Joan Fox

Joan had five brothers and sisters. Andy Jr. was 27 and, after serving in Vietnam, had become a police officer in New Jersey. Myrtle was next oldest and then came Linda, aged 21. Raymond was 19 and at the time was serving in Vietnam, Joan was 17, and Ruthie, the youngest, was aged 15. Joan was born in Philadelphia, and moved with her family to the New Jersey suburbs in the 1950s when she was three.

Joan was always boy-crazy. She began dating Craig early in high school. Though they occasionally had arguments and would go off and date other people, they always came back together and as time went on they grew closer. Joan became increasingly dependent on Craig, and her friends felt that she was obsessed with him. During one brief break-up in the summer of 1968, Joan wrote to a friend, "I get so afraid I'm going to lose him, I don't know what I'm ever going to do..." (Asinof 1971).

Joan had to deal with a squabbling family at home. She also had to deal with contradictions in her life; the urge to succeed and be popular led her to become a cheerleader, and this was at odds with her more serious and thoughtful side.

The Last Year

At that time, Blackwood was a very conventional middle-class community, but even so there were a handful of thoughtful, more free-minded students who were part of what we now call the 1960s culture. They opposed the war in Vietnam, they smoked marijuana, and they questioned conventional culture. Craig and Joan were friends with this group of students. They also had friends who could be considered mainstream, small-town Americans.

Eventually both Craig and Joan, but especially Craig, began to change their attitudes: they opposed the war and the intolerance and small-mindedness of society. In the fall of 1968, Craig and Joan had marched to Camden to support American soldiers in Vietnam. Then Craig visited Philadelphia to join a more avant-garde group. His views began to change more and more. As he sought out the few students at the high school with more modern ideas, he had to deal with a great deal of conflict, both at home with his family and within himself. Because his family did not agree with his opinions, he was forced to call friends from a pay phone to discuss his views.

Although the arrival of his brother Bernie and his family forced Craig out of his own room, he seemed to enjoy their company. Bernie saw that Craig needed to get away from home, but a plan to go to North Carolina for the summer fell through. On his 17th birthday, his father bought Craig a 1962 Falcon.

In the summer of 1969, Craig and Joan worked at a music fair. They had fun at first, but soon got depressed by the superficiality and pettiness of the world of show business. Joan also worked in a program for kids at the Methodist Church, and they both began to consider joining the Peace Corps after high school. Craig spent a lot of time that summer reading and writing poems, and his notebooks indicate a growing confusion and sadness.

Asinof presents a gloomy picture of the Highland High School in Blackwood. At that time, Blackwood was a town that had not produced any distinguished people. The town was run by building contractors, and the richest men were a building contractor and a funeral director. The school was newly built in 1967, but by 1969 the walls were cracking and the floors buckling. The school administration was concerned with discipline rather than education. It had twice as many gym teachers as social studies teachers, and as many shop teachers as English teachers. One year after it opened, the students spontaneously revolted and picketed the school. As a result the five-minute period between classes was extended to eight minutes. The school rewarded compliance. In 1968, a straw poll among the students gave George Wallace 38 percent of the votes for President and Nixon 34 percent. The student body sent CARE packages to American soldiers in Vietnam.

Craig was without direction. He liked the theater but felt he had limitations that would prevent success. He could go to Glassboro State College, but really didn't know what he would do there. He had no special talents or inclinations. The Peace Corps seemed to be the only option. He kidded around much less that fall and his friends noticed how much more serious he had become.

Craig and Joan, who had become lovers earlier that spring, became inseparable. Craig seemed to really want her, and Joan needed him. Friends thought that she was beginning to lose her self-identity. Joan was now a cheerleader, and Craig was planning a production of *The Mouse That Roared*, but they began to withdraw from their friends. Craig stayed in his room a lot by himself, depressed, writing sad poems.

When the idea for Moratorium Day on October 15, 1969, was first publicized, Craig and Joan were enthusiastic, though the school administrators forbade any demonstration and threatened to punish any students who cut school that day.

Craig talked about it a lot at home and tried to persuade his parents to take his side on the issue.

On the Sunday before Moratorium Day, Craig fixed the tail pipe on his car. He snapped at his brother for borrowing his car. Bernie was surprised because Craig never got angry at little things like that. On Tuesday afternoon, Craig wrote letters and cleaned out his room. He cleaned out his desk and burned all of his notebooks in the incinerator in the back yard, together with all the posters that he had taken off the walls of his room. He had already given his sister-in-law his loose change as a gift for his nephew.

Craig and Joan went to the rally at Glassboro State College on Wednesday, but the lack of organization and lack of real feeling depressed them. They drove home in the mid-afternoon. He dropped Joan off at home and planned to pick her up at 7 p.m.

After meeting Joan, instead of driving to the candlelight march at Glassboro, they drove to a wooded lane where Craig connected a vacuum cleaner hose to the tail pipe and then through a hole that he had drilled in the floor of the car. Both were later found dead, victims of carbon monoxide poisoning.

CASE DISCUSSION

Most observers felt that the decision to die was Craig's. He was depressed over life in general and the government's involvement in Vietnam in particular. He wanted to die, and Joan had said that if he wanted to die, so did she. Certainly Craig had been depressed in the months before his suicide, though the focus of his depression was unclear.

Bernie thought that Craig suffered because Bernie was clearly his father's favorite. Bernie stole the glory in the family, and the things that Craig liked to do were seen as sissy-like. Craig had been a fat kid, while Bernie was a fine athlete. When Bernie came home to stay, he drove Craig out of his own room. Perhaps Craig felt that he wasn't really loved.

In one letter that was revealed, Craig wrote to a friend:

...My life is complete except all my brothers are in trouble — war, poverty, hunger, hostility. My purpose is to make them understand all this trouble. Maybe this will start a chain reaction of awakening, love, communication. I've been so down, so goddam down, I can't get up. Not even pot helps... (Asinof 1971).

In a letter to her mother, Joan said that they wanted to be martyrs. She did not think that what they were planning was cowardly or that they were copping out. They believed deeply in what they were doing.

This case is a puzzle — an enigma. Neither Craig nor Joan showed any signs of psychiatric disturbance prior to their suicide. Craig was depressed, but no evaluation can be made as to how severely depressed he was or what the exact psychiatric nature of his depression was. Their stated motive for dying was for the cause of peace. But could they really believe that their death would achieve peace?

REFERENCES

Asinof, E. 1971. *Craig and Joan*. New York: Viking.

Fishbain, D.A. and T.E. Aldrich. 1985. Suicide pacts. *Journal of Clinical Psychiatry* 46:11-15.

Rosenbaum, M. 1983. Crime and punishment. *Archives of General Psychiatry* 40:979-982.

Wickett, A. 1989. *Double Exit*. Eugene, OR: Hemlock Society.

Chapter 10

A Deviant Theory of
Adolescent Suicide

It is a common misperception that improvements in the quality of life lead to a happier or more contented individual. If people have a higher standard of living, more personal possessions, more income, more education, better physical health, and more leisure time, then their psychological health surely ought to be better. It seems that this is not always the case. An example of why and how better life conditions do not necessarily constitute better mental health can be found in the study of suicide.

SUICIDE RATES AND THE QUALITY OF LIFE

Is suicide, as many contend, a response to unpleasant and painful life situations? Henry and Short (1954) agreed that suicide is more likely to occur when people are unhappy but they claim that it occurs mainly when people have no outside source to blame for their misery. If an external source of blame exists, then people can blame their misery on that outside source. When this is the case, people are more likely to become angry and assaultive (and, in the extreme, homicidal) and less likely to become depressed and suicidal.

The common-sense hypothesis and Henry and Short's hypothesis lead to opposite predictions. Common sense suggests that as the quality of life improves suicide should become less common. Henry and Short's theory, on the other hand, suggests that, as the quality of life improves, suicide should become more common and murder less common.

Put differently, if an external source of blame exists for one's misery, such as religious persecution, political oppression, racism or poverty, then people can easily attribute their misery to this clear external source of frustration. Therefore, they are more likely to be angry and, in the extreme, assaultive.

On the other hand, if the quality of life improves and one is *still* unhappy, then there is no longer any clear external source of frustration on which to blame one's misery. The better the quality of life, the more likely it is that one's misery will be seen as an inevitable consequence of life itself and, perhaps, one's own dysfunctional personality. Therefore, people in this condition are more likely to become depressed and suicidal.

Lester (1984a) tested these opposing hypotheses using a sample from 43 nations of the world. In 1984, Estes tested these nations for their quality of life. Lester found that the suicide rate in each respective nation was associated with the quality of life. Conversely, homicide rates were lower in nations with a higher quality of life.

In subsequent research, Lester (1984b) found the same phenomenon when the quality of life in the American states was studied; suicide rates were higher and homicide rates were lower in those states with a higher quality of life.

The notion that suicidal behavior, in contrast to homicidal behavior, is more likely when the distressed individual has no external source to blame can be extended to other kinds of external frustrations as well (Lester 1970).

EXTERNAL STRESS

No satisfactory explanation has ever been proposed for why suicide rates are higher on the west coast of America than they are on the east coast. Perhaps the milder west coast weather causes fewer external sources of frustration on which people can focus their distress (such as less ice, snow, cold temperatures and pot holes). If people experience some degree of malaise or depression during winter, their feelings can more easily be attributed to external frustrations on the east coast than on the west coast.

This hypothesis might also be used to explain the supposedly low rate of suicide found among victims of the Nazi concentration camps (Kwiet 1984); they had a clear external source to blame for their misery.

Removal of External Stress

Removal of external stress should lead to an increase in the suicide rate since its elimination will make it increasingly difficult to refer feelings of distress and depression to external frustrations. This hypothesis could account for the fact that suicide rates increase after a war ends, after winter ends (suicide rates peak in the spring), and after a divorce.

Removal of Personal Stress

Removal of personal stress may also lead to an increased likelihood of suicidal behavior. For example, compared with the suicide rate during pregnancy, the post-partum suicide rate should be high and it is. The suicide rate is also higher for individuals with a corrected deformity or corrected congenital defect such as blindness. Suicide may also be more likely after a change of job, position at work, residence, or friends. In each case, a circumstance that might have accounted for one's misery is removed and, if the misery continues, it will not be as easy to externalize the blame for the misery.

This is the "if only" syndrome. "If only I had a new spouse, car, house, job, etc., then everything would be wonderful." Unfortunately, after the new house or job is obtained, life often continues to be terrible. The grass turns out not to be greener on the other side; it is merely a different shade of brown.

ADOLESCENT PROBLEMS

Many writers claim that life today is more difficult for adolescents than it was in the past. Uhlenberg and Eggebeen (1986), however, noted that the social conditions of adolescents have improved in recent years. From 1960 to 1980 they documented a reduction in poverty, smaller families, more educated parents, better schools, and increased expenditures on social welfare for children. However, they also noted that SAT scores have declined, delinquency has increased, drug and alcohol abuse have become more common, illegitimate births have increased, and violent deaths (suicide and homicide) have become more common.

Uhlenberg and Eggebeen were surprised by their findings and blamed poorer parenting in recent years for the decline in the well-being of adolescents. From another perspective, however, these results are not surprising, but expected. Uhlenberg and Eggebeen's use of the concept of "well-being" is ambiguous. Social conditions may have improved, increasing the social well-being of adolescents, but personal adjustment may have worsened, as Henry and Short would predict, decreasing the psychological well-being of adolescents.

For adolescents today the life conditions are remarkably better than in previous years. Adolescents now have increased material wealth, better health, and increased leisure time. Compare the lives of your children today with those of your parents or grandparents.

My own parents, for instance, were forced to leave school

at the age of 12 because their families needed their income. My mother worked as a hotel maid, six days a week for long hours. My father worked as a clerk in an accounting office. They did not get their teeth straightened, they were not immunized against childhood diseases and, as both were the fourth child of five, they never got new clothes or toys.

My son, on the other hand, went to a parochial school, had his own telephone line at the house, built up a $3000 baseball card collection, dressed well and had the best health care. As a society our opinions about what constitutes a good life have changed dramatically. For adolescents today, a telephone, a television and fancy sneakers are now considered necessities.

DISCUSSION

The thesis proposed in this chapter is heresy. Nevertheless, it may have some merit. It proposes that as the quality of life improves for people, including adolescents, suicide may become more common. Problems cannot be avoided simply by improving education, health care and working conditions, and then sitting back to enjoy the fruits of the improved quality of life. At that stage, people may begin to experience psychological problems that are quite different from those that existed in the past, but equally serious.

The problems typically presented by disturbed people in the early part of this century, such as those treated by Sigmund Freud, have become less common. Today, clients are more likely to complain to their psychotherapists about feeling bored, unfulfilled and having a lack of meaning in their life. Thus, as the quality of life improves, it is important to be alert for signs of psychological distress such as depression and suicidal preoccupation. Likewise, activity programs for people, especially adolescents, must be devised that will contribute meaningful and fulfilling experiences to their lives.

The solutions differ for everyone. However, meaning is often derived from being active and involved. We need to involve adolescents in activities, to encourage them to participate in athletics or to do volunteer work and help others in the community. Too often, youths (and adults) select sedentary activities, such as watching television, playing video games, and taking alcohol and drugs. These activities simply fill time and do not help give meaning to life. Indeed, one very important goal for education, other than preparing people for careers, may be to prepare people to enjoy their leisure time and to find meaning in their lives.

REFERENCES

Estes, R.J. 1984. *The Social Progress of Nations*. New York: Praeger.

Henry, A.F. and J.F. Short. 1954. *Suicide and Homicide*. New York: Free Press.

Kwiet, K. 1984. The ultimate refuge. *Leo Baeck Institute Yearbook* 29:135-168.

Lester, D. 1970. Suicidal behavior and external constraints. *Psychological Reports* 27:777-778.

Lester, D. 1984a. The association between the quality of life and suicide and homicide rates. *Journal of Social Psychology* 124:247-248.

Lester, D. 1984b. The quality of life and suicide. *Journal of Social Psychology* 125:279-280.

Uhlenberg, P. and D. Eggebeen, D. 1986. The declining well-being of American adolescents. *The Public Interest* 82:25-38.

Chapter 11

Assessing Suicidality in Adolescents: A Chapter for the Professional

The assessment of suicidality in adolescents is critically dependent upon the answers to three questions: (1) what is the source of the adolescents who are to be assessed, (2) what is the purpose of the assessment, and (3) what is to be assessed? Let us consider each of these in turn.

THE SOURCE OF THE ADOLESCENTS

Adolescents needing assessment may be found in institutions, including schools, juvenile delinquent facilities, shelters for runaways, psychiatric clinics and from teen hotlines, to name just a few. The adolescents found in these institutions are different from one another in many ways and no single set of assessment procedures can suffice for all adolescents in all institutions. The problem is further complicated by the fact that regional differences exist. In other words, adolescents found in psychiatric clinics in one country or state may differ considerably from those found in psychiatric clinics else-where. The ideal solution—that each clinic devise its own assessment procedures that are carefully tailored to its own adolescent population—requires hiring a skilled psychological researcher and having a large adolescent clientele on whom to develop and validate an assessment procedure. Of course, this is usually not practical, and therefore institutions have to make use of assessment procedures developed by others.

THE PURPOSE OF THE ASSESSMENT

The second issue concerns the purpose of the assessment procedure. It is of critical importance for an institution to know if an adolescent has attempted suicide, or is preoccupied by suicide. In some cases assessment may serve little practical purpose. For example, very few psychotherapists find it neces-sary to administer psychological tests to their clients in order to provide good psychotherapy. Psychotherapists usually find that after having several sessions with the client, they acquire sufficient information to formulate a treatment plan. Also, some institutions that administer to juvenile delinquents, pro-vide such minimal mental health services that assessment is not always practical. However, assessment of every adolescent *upon admission* to any psychiatric facility is critical and should be conducted even if it is cursory. If no one knows that a person is suicidal, precautions to prevent the loss of life will not be taken.

There is one other very important reason to ensure that adequate assessment occurs—the threat of lawsuits. If an ado-lescent commits suicide while in treatment or while confined, that institution is responsible and will most likely lose the case if it is brought to court. Institutions must be able to show that they followed appropriate assessment procedures and used the resulting information wisely if they have any hope for winning a lawsuit. Also, because most parents feel responsible for their children, especially if they are still minors, it is more probable that they will sue the institution in which their child committed suicide.

THE FOCUS OF THE ASSESSMENT

The third issue concerns the focus of the assessment. Of course, it is important to assess the suicidality of an adolescent, but treatment procedures are not normally dependent upon the *suicidality* of the adolescent. The treatment chosen is determined more by the psychiatric diagnosis and the family and social situation of the adolescent. For example, the treatment plan will typically focus on how to alleviate the adolescent's depression or how to improve relationships in his family. The degree of suicidality merely determines the urgency with which some treatment procedures are pursued (Should the adolescent be hospitalized immediately in a psychiatric institution?) and which custodial procedures might need to be undertaken. For example, should the adolescent be placed in a suicide-proof environment and monitored continuously?

THE ASSESSMENT OF SUICIDALITY

In the 1950s, the Los Angeles Suicide Prevention Center developed a simple suicidality assessment instrument for use by counselors on their clients. This scale still forms the basis for most suicidality assessment in suicide prevention centers, and it has some relevance here. A shortened version of this scale (prepared by Kenneth Whittemore; see Lester 1989) is shown in Figure 11-1.

Figure 11-1.

A Suicide Prevention Center Suicide Potential Scale

Name:_____ Age:_____ Sex:____

Date:_____

Rater:_____ Evaluation: 1 2 3 4 5 6 7 8 9

L   M   H

This schedule attempts to rate suicide potentiality. By suicide potentiality is meant generally the possibility that the person might destroy himself, in the present or immediate future. Listed below are categories with descriptive items which have been found to be useful in evaluating suicide potentiality. The numbers in parentheses after each item suggest the most common range of values or weights to be assigned that item: 9 is the highest, or most seriously suicidal, while 1 is the lowest, or the least seriously suicidal. The rating assigned will depend on the individual case. The rater will note the range of ratings assigned to each item varies.

The rating for each of the five categories is the average of the rates assigned to the total number of items ranked within that category. (Seldom will one be able to rate every item.)

The overall suicide potentiality rating may be found by entering the weights assigned for each category below, totaling, and dividing by the number of categories rated. This number, rounded to the nearest whole number, should also be circled at the top of this page. It is this number (circled above) which represents the degree of lethality of the person being evaluated.

Category	*Rating*
A. Age and Sex	____
B. Symptoms	____
C. Stress	____
D. Prior suicidal behavior and current plan	____
E. Communication aspects, resources, and reaction of significant other(s)	____
Total	____
Divide by number of categories rated	____
Average (round to nearest whole number and circle at top of page)	____

A. **Age and Sex (1-9)**   **Rating for Category**
    Males

    1. 50 plus (7-9)   ____
    2. 35-49 (5-7)   ____
    3. 15-34 (3-5)   ____

    Females

    4. All ages (1-3)   ____

B. **Symptoms (1-9)**

    5. Severe depression: sleep disorder, anorexia,
        weight loss, withdrawal, despondent, loss of
        interest, apathy (7-9)   ____
    6. Feelings of hopelessness, helplessness and
        exhaustion (7-9)   ____
    7. Disorganization, confusion, chaos, delusions,
        hallucination, loss of contact, disorientation (6-8)   ____
    8. Alcoholism, drug addiction, homosexuality,
        compulsive gambling (4-8)   ____
    9. Agitation, tension, anxiety (4-6)   ____
    10. Guilt, shame, embarrassment (4-6)   ____
    11. Feelings of rage, hostility, anger, revenge,
         jealousy (4-6)   ____
    12. Poor impulse control, poor judgment (4-6)   ____
    13. Chronic debilitating illness (5-7)   ____
    14. Repeated unsuccessful experiences with
         doctors and/or therapists (4-6)   ____
    15. Psychosomatic illness (asthma, ulcer, etc.)
         and/or hypochondria (chronic minor illness
         complaints) (1-4)   ____

C. **Stress and Its Occurrence (Acute vs. Chronic) (1-9)**
    16. Loss of loved person by death, divorce, or
         separation (including possible long-term
         hospitalization, etc.) (5-9)   ____
    17. Loss of job, money, prestige, status (4-8)   ____
    18. Sickness, serious illness, surgery, accident,
         loss of limb (3-7)   ____
    19. Threat of prosecution, criminal involvement,
         exposure (4-6)   ____
    20. Change(s) in life, environment, setting (4-6) ____
    21. Sharp, noticeable, and sudden onset of
         specific stress/symptoms (1-9)   ____

22. Recurrent outbreak of similar symptoms
    and/or stress (4-9)   ____
23. Recent increase in long-standing traits,
    symptoms/stress (4-7)   ____

D. Prior Suicidal Behavior and Current Plan (1-9)

24. Rated lethality of previous attempts (1-9)   ____
25. History of repeated threats and depression (3-5)   ____
26. Specificity of current plan and lethality of
    proposed method — aspirin, pills, poison,
    knife, drowning, hanging, jump, gun (1-9)   ____
27. Availability of means in proposed method
    and specificity in time planned (1-9)   ____

**E. Resources, Communication Aspects, and Reaction
of Significant Other(s)* (1-9)**

28. No sources of financial support (employment,
    agencies, family) (4-9)   ____
29. No personal emotional support — family and/or
    friends — available, unwilling to help (4-7)   ____
30. Communication broken with rejection of efforts
    to re-establish by both patient and others (5-7)   ____
31. Communications have internalized goal, e.g.
    declaration of guilt, feelings of worthlessness,
    blame, shame (4-7)   ____
32. Communications have interpersonalized goal,
    e.g. to cause guilt in others, to force action
    in others, etc. (2-4)   ____

Reaction of Significant Other(s) *

33. Defensive, paranoid, rejecting, punishing
    attitude (5-7)   ____
34. Denial of own or patient's need for help (5-7)   ____
35. No feeling of concern about the patient, doesn't
    understand the patient (4-6)   ____
36. Indecisive or alternating attitude-feelings of anger
    and rejection and of responsibility and desire to help
                                                 (2-5) ____

*Answers gained by direct contact with the significant other(s)
are often more reliable than those gained from the patient himself.

This scale has five sections. The first section (A) is concerned with age and sex; when the scale was developed, completed suicide was most common in elderly white males. Clearly, the relevance of age in this scale needs to be modified because the target population is young, and because there has been such a dramatic increase in the rates of adolescent suicide since the scale was developed (Maris 1985).

The second section of the scale (B) focuses on the type and severity of psychiatric disturbance. Suicide risk is greater in those with psychosis, in substance abusers, and in those who are seriously depressed. These guidelines are probably valid for all populations, including adolescents (Spirito et al. 1989). One issue that must be addressed specifically for adolescents is the accurate diagnosis of depression, since some clinicians have suggested that depression may be "masked" in adolescents and manifested only by atypical symptoms.

The third section (C) of the suicide assessment scale refers to recent stressors in the person's life, including losses of significant others, jobs, money, prestige, and status. Other stressors are illness, accidents, criminal activity, and changes in residence. The more recent the stress, the greater the risk of suicide, especially if a person's stress level has shown a recent increase on top of an already high level.

The fourth section (D) concerns suicidal behavior. If a person has recently attempted suicide, especially using a method of high lethality, if the person has a specific plan for committing suicide in the future, and if the method of choice is readily available, then the risk of future suicidal behavior is especially high. People who are not used to working with suicidal clients are often reluctant to ask clients questions about these types of behaviors and plans, but this information is critical to an adequate evaluation of suicidal risk. Also, *there is no evidence that asking a client about suicidal preoccupation will increase the chance that that client will commit suicide.*

Finally, the fifth section of the scale (E) inquires about the availability of resources and support for the person and the attitude of those able to provide support. For example, are the client's significant others hostile or sympathetic?

Few of the telephone counselors at suicide prevention

centers are able to actually complete an accurate evaluation of the suicidality of each caller, but the areas of concern covered in the scale are typically covered during the course of a conversation with a client. Thus, if need be, the counselor could complete the "Suicide Potential Scale" on a client after they got off the phone.

Lettieri (1974) derived separate scales for predicting suicide in younger males, older males, younger females, and older females, but somehow his scales did not receive wide acceptance, and researchers have not pursued his idea of deriving separate scales for different demographic groups.

RECOMMENDATIONS FOR ADOLESCENT ASSESSMENT

Recently, Garrison and his collaborators (1991) reviewed assessment instruments that had been used to study suicidal adolescents. (For a more detailed description of this survey and the instruments, see Lewinsohn et al. [1989].) Of those instruments reviewed for the direct assessment of suicidality, the Suicidal Ideation Questionnaire (Reynolds 1987) is one of the few developed specifically for adolescents and that contains adequate norms and information on reliability and validity. More recently, Reynolds (1990) also developed a semi-structured clinical interview to inquire about and assess suicidal behavior in adolescents.

The association between depression and suicidality found in adults has been found to be true for adolescents as well (Spirito et al. 1989). Therefore, the assessment of depression is most important. There are several instruments devised for assessing depression especially for adolescents, such as the Reynolds Adolescent Depression Scale (Reynolds 1986). This scale has adequate norms and well-established reliability and validity. There are also alternative scales that can be utilized such as Kovac's (1985).

Beck and his co-workers (1974) found that one particular component of the set of depressive symptoms that is very strongly associated with prior, current and future suicidality

are feelings of hopelessness. The association between hopelessness and suicidality is often found to be stronger than the
association between depression and suicidality. Spirito's team
(1989) found evidence that hopelessness is strongly associated
with suicidality in adolescents, too. Therefore, it is useful to
assess hopelessness as well as depression in potentially suicidal adolescents. Scales have been developed to assess depression specifically for adolescents, such as Kazdin and his
co-workers (1986). The properties of their scale have been
evaluated, and it appears to be useful in working with suicidal
adolescents (Spirito et al. 1988).

Finally, there are several scales that assess the magnitude
of recent stressors (Holmes and Rahe 1967; Sarason et al. 1978),
and some of these are oriented toward adolescents in particular
(Johnson and McCutcheon 1980).

OTHER AREAS TO EXPLORE IN THE ASSESSMENT OF ADOLESCENT SUICIDALITY

Research findings on suicidality in adolescents can help sensitize the clinician to the risk factors that are important to cover
in an assessment. Simple epidemiological studies indicate that
suicide is related to age, sex and race. Although very young
children can show suicidal behavior (Berman 1991), its frequency increases around the time of puberty. Male adolescents
have a higher risk of *completed* suicide, at least in the United
States, but *attempted* suicide is usually more common among
female adolescents. White adolescents have the highest risk of
suicide; Hispanic youths have a high rate in some regions of
the United States such as the Southwest; African American
youths in certain cities and Native American youths in some
reservations have high rates of suicide. It is, therefore, useful
for clinicians to be aware of the epidemiological trends for
youth suicide in their locale. Other risk factors include:

1. *Psychiatric Disorders*
    As discussed in earlier chapters, suicidal behavior is

more common in those who are psychiatrically disturbed. The majority of adolescents who are suicidal can be given a psychiatric diagnosis (Shafii et al. 1985), though many of them are either not in treatment or not responding to treatment. We presented a case of this type (Michael Wechsler) in the first chapter. Therefore, accurate diagnosis and appropriate treatment for the psychiatric disorder are crucial for all potentially suicidal youths. Although treatment does not always prevent youths from killing themselves, the chance that intervention can occur will be greater if the youth is in treatment.

2. *Historical and Situational Risk Factors*
We have noted that several risk factors from the adolescent's life history and current situation are important to look for, such as poor academic performance and specific skill deficits (Rourke et al. 1989; Lester 1992). In adults these factors are perhaps analogous to unemployment, marriage or job difficulties. Chronic and debilitating illnesses are less common in adolescents than they are in adults and, therefore, when they are present in adolescents they become more significant as suicide risk factors. Also, poor relationships with peers and involvement with other depressed and alienated friends (Lester 1987) are also risk factors for adolescents.

The adolescent's family provides important sources of suicidal motivation for adolescents. Psychiatrically disturbed parents increase the risk of suicide in their children, especially if depression and a family history of suicide are present. Such a family history suggests the possibility of a genetically transmitted psychiatric disorder and this increases the likelihood of a dysfunctional family environment and provides a coping style for the children to imitate.

In the 1980s, a great deal of research implicated physical and sexual abuse of children by parents as a significant factor in increasing the risk of psychological disturbance and suicide risk in adolescents (Lester

1992). These experiences are especially common in children who run away from home and who are in shelters. Jacobs (1971) also documented the chaotic family environments of suicidal adolescents; the mother may marry and divorce several times or the family may frequently change residence. As noted before, an increase in stressful life events above and beyond an already stressful life is an important warning sign for suicidality.

One other factor to look for that is perhaps unique to assessing suicidal risk in adolescents is the presence of risky and mildly self-destructive and self-defeating behavior, especially in male adolescents (Lester and Gatto 1989).

3. *Psychological Factors*
    As noted above, suicidality is frequently associated with depression and hopelessness. In children and adolescents, the depression is sometimes "masked," that is, not manifest in the signs typically shown by depressed adults. For example, Greene and Keown (1986) presented the case of a 12-year-old boy who was hospitalized after taking 20 acetaminophen tablets. The mother had recently remarried and moved the family to a new city. In the new school the boy's grades dropped from B's to D's. He fought with the other boys at school and was suspended. The boy's behavioral problems were signs of depression, and this sort of acting-out behavior is common in depressed adolescents.

    Depressed adolescents may be irritable, unreasonably angry, and antisocial. They may experience wild mood swings, complain of boredom and may run away from home. Girls may become sexually promiscuous and boys may fight and commit acts of vandalism. On the other hand, accurate self-reporting of depression is not uncommon, and indeed Lester (1990) has found that adolescents in high school report much higher levels of depression on self-report inventories than do college students.

Research in the 1980s identified borderline personality disorder traits as being strongly associated with suicidality (Lester 1992). Impulsivity and anger have also been implicated. The impulsivity of suicidal adolescents is perhaps responsible for their susceptibility to feeling suicidal after celebrities commit suicide (Stack 1990), if someone in their neighborhood or school has recently committed suicide (Coleman 1987), and for becoming suicidal after experiencing losses that an adult observer might not seem especially severe. The possibility of the occurrence of suicidal "epidemics" in schools after an adolescent has attempted or completed a suicide has led to many suggestions for preventing such contagion (Leenaars and Wenckstern 1991).

Finally, low self-esteem has been found to be common in suicidal adolescents and has been found to predict subsequent suicidal behavior (Kaplan and Pokorny 1976).

THE SOURCE OF THE ADOLESCENTS TO BE ASSESSED

As mentioned at the beginning of this chapter, the source of the adolescents (or the institution in which they may be found) plays a role in determining what assessment procedures are appropriate.

For example, Hendren and Blumenthal (1989) have discussed assessment in the forensic setting, in other words, adolescents who come to the attention of the criminal justice system (such as law enforcement agencies). Hendren and Blumenthal listed the following risk factors for adolescent suicide:

- a history of suicidal threats and attempts
- drug or alcohol abuse
- depression
- antisocial behavior
- an inhibited personality
- direct or indirect exposure to suicide

- evidence of family dysfunction
- anniversary of a negative life event
- recent stressors or losses

It is likely that all adolescents, both suicidal and nonsuicidal, who come to the attention of police officers are apt to have more of these risk factors than other adolescents. Thus, are police officers to consider most of the adolescents they encounter as potentially suicidal?

Interestingly, Hendren and Blumenthal do not answer this question. The risk factors they list are those used for adolescents in general and are not tailored to the special subgroup that their article addresses. Their paper, therefore, simply serves to acquaint readers with the general problems of assessing the risk of suicide in adolescents. Similar criticisms can be made of papers that address adolescent suicide in schools and in particular ethnic groups such as Hispanics and native Americans.

Gibson (1989) has provided a more focused discussion that addresses the problem of suicidality in gay and lesbian youths. In addition to the typical risk factors, he added factors related to homosexual orientation: denial of homosexual desires; rejection and harassment by parents, relatives and peers because of the homosexuality; involuntary treatment to change the homosexual orientation; social isolation and inability to meet others like themselves; guilt over being homosexual, internalization of the societal image of homosexuals as sick; and problems in their homosexual relationships.

However, much more research needs to be done on the correlates of suicidal risk in adolescents from different settings and institutions so that we can identify risk factors unique to these different populations.

THE CLINICAL INTERVIEW

In any assessment procedure, it is important for the clinician to establish a good relationship with the client, and in the case of an adolescent this should include both the client and the family members. The clinician should gather all necessary information and, if he is going to continue to be the adolescent's psychotherapist, he should begin to develop a therapeutic alliance at the time of the assessment.

Adolescents present special problems for the clinician since they are more likely than adults to have difficulty verbalizing their thoughts and feelings. The clinician must, therefore, adapt the interview to the adolescent's maturity and style, and some examples of such interviews have been provided by Fremouw and his team (1990).

Adolescents may be less willing than adults to trust the clinician. This distrust is perhaps understandable since in many cases the parents or teachers insists that an adolescent see a clinician and this may immediately put the youngster on guard. Also, because the interviewer is often an agent for and paid by the parents or the state (Halleck 1972) he may not necessarily have the adolescent's best interests at heart. Many years ago Greist and his co-workers (1973) developed a computer-administered interview for suicide risk assessment, and they found that many clients preferred the computer-administered interview to one administered by a clinician. This technique should be developed further, incorporating more recent information about suicidal risk assessment, for it might prove useful with some highly resistant adolescents.

CONCLUSIONS

It has been noted in this chapter that the assessment of suicidal risk in adolescents must encompass two needs. First, clinicians must acquire all of the information necessary to plan an adequate treatment program for the adolescent and to assess the urgency with which suicide prevention measures must be undertaken. Planning a treatment program requires a general assessment of the psychiatric state and the social situation of the adolescent. Deciding the urgency with which treatment should commence and whether suicide precautions are warranted requires that the assessment focus on the prediction of suicide risk. It is important that clinicians acquaint themselves with appropriate guidelines for the assessment and management of suicidal adolescents, such as those recently published by Fremouw and co-workers (1990).

Secondly, clinicians must be sure that they have met adequate clinical and legal standards of care, in both the assessment and the management of the potentially suicidal adolescent. An excellent in-depth discussion of these standards has recently been presented by Bongar (1991). Failure to meet the appropriate standards may result in the clinician losing civil suits brought by the family of an adolescent who commits suicide, civil suits which may be costly for the clinician both in financial terms and in the psychological distress caused by the unfortunate suicide of a client followed by the anger of the family.

REFERENCES

Beck, A.T., A. Weissman, D. Lester, D. and L. Trexler. 1974. The measurement of pessimism. *Journal of Consulting and Clinical Psychology* 42:861-865.

Berman, A.L. 1991. Case consultation: David. *Suicide and Life-Threatening Behavior* 21:299-306.

Bongar, B. 1991. *The Suicidal Patient: Clinical and Legal Standards of Care*. Washington, DC: American Psychological Association.

Coleman, L. 1987. *Suicide Clusters*. Boston: Faber & Faber.

Fremouw, W.J., M. de Perczel and T.E. Ellis. 1990. *Suicide Risk: Assessment and Response Guidelines*. New York: Pergamon.

Garrison, C.Z., P.M. Lewinsohn, F. Marsteller, J. Langhinrichsen and I. Lann. 1991. The assessment of suicidal behavior in adolescents. *Suicide and Life-Threatening Behavior* 21:217-230.

Gibson, P. 1989. Gay male and lesbian youth suicide. In *The Report of the Secretary's Task Force on Youth Suicide*, Vol. 3. Washington, DC: US Government Printing Office.

Greene, J.W. and M. Keown, M. 1986. Depression and suicide in children and adolescents. *Comprehensive Therapy* 12(2):38-43.

Greist, J., D. Gustafson, D., F. Strauss, F.G. Rowse, T. Laughren and J. Chiles. 1973. A computer interview for suicide risk prediction. *American Journal of Psychiatry* 130:1327-1332.

Halleck, S. 1972. *The Politics of Therapy*. New York: Harper & Row.

Hendren, R.L. and S.J. Blumenthal. 1989. Adolescent suicide. *Forensic Reports* 2:47-63.

Holmes, T.H. and R.H. Rahe. 1967. The social readjustment scale. *Journal of Psychosomatic Research* 11:213-218.

Jacobs, J. 1971. *Adolescent Suicide*. New York: Wiley.

Johnson, J.H. and S. McCutcheon.1980. Assessing life stress in older children and adolescents. In I.D. Sarason and C.D. Spielberger, eds., *Stress and Anxiety*, Vol. 7. Washington, DC: Hemisphere.

Kaplan, H. and A.D. Pokorny. 1976. Self-derogation and suicide. *Social Science and Medicine* 10:113-121.

Kazdin, A.E. A. Rodgas and D. Colbus. 1986. The hopelessness scale for children. *Journal of Consulting and Clinical Psychology* 54:241-245.

Kovacs, M. 1985. The Children's Depression Inventory. *Psychopharmacology Bulletin* 21:995-998.

Leenaars, A.A. and S. Wenckstern. 1991. *Suicide Prevention in Schools*. Washington, DC: Hemisphere.

Lester, D. 1987. A subcultural theory of teenage suicide. *Adolescence* 22:317-320.

Lester, D. 1989. *Can We Prevent Suicide?* New York: AMS.

Lester, D. 1990. Depression and suicide in college students. *Personality and Individual Differences* 11:757-758.

Lester, D. 1992. *Why People Kill Themselves*, 3rd Ed. Springfield, IL: Charles C Thomas.

Lester, D. and J.L. Gatto. 1989. Self-destructive tendencies and depression as predictors of suicidal ideation in teenagers. *Journal of Adolescence* 12:221-223.

Lettieri, D.J. 1974. Suicidal death prediction scales. In A. T. Beck, H.L.P. Resnik and D.J. Lettieri, eds., *The Prediction of Suicide*. Philadelphia: The Charles Press.

Lewinsohn, P.M., C.Z. Garrison, J. Langhinrichsen and F. Marsteller. 1989. *The Assessment of Suicidal Behavior in Adolescents*. Rockville, MD: National Institute of Mental Health.

Maris, R. 1985. The adolescent suicide problem. *Suicide and Life-Threatening Behavior* 15:91-109.

Reynolds, W.M. 1986. *The Reynolds Adolescent Depression Scale*. Odessa, FL: Psychological Assessment Resources.

Reynolds, W.M. 1987. *The Suicidal Ideation Questionnaire*. Odessa, FL: Psychological Assessment Resources.

Reynolds, W.M. 1990. Development of a semistructured clinical interview for suicidal behaviors in adolescents. *Psychological Assessment* 2:382-390.

Rourke, B., G. Young and A. Leenaars. 1989. A childhood learning disability that predisposes those afflicted to adolescent and adult depression and suicide risk. *Journal of Learning Disabilities* 22:169-175.

Sarason, I., J. Johnson and J. Siegel, J. 1978. Assessing the impact of life changes. *Journal of Consulting and Clinical Psychology* 46:932-946.

Shafii, M., S. Carrigan, J. Whittinghill and A. Derrick. 1985. Psychological autopsy of completed suicide in children and adolescents. *American Journal of Psychiatry* 142:1061-1064.

Spirito, A., L. Brown, J. Overholser and G. Fritz. 1989. Attempted suicide in adolescence. *Clinical Psychology Review* 9:335-363.

Spirito, A., C.A. Williams, L.J. Stark and K. J. Hart. 1988. The hopelessness scale for children. *Journal of Abnormal Child Psychology* 16:445-458.

Stack, S. 1990. Media impacts on suicide. In D. Lester, ed., *Current Concepts of Suicide*. Philadelphia: The Charles Press.

Chapter 12

Treatment and Therapy

The answer to the question of how best to help the suicidal adolescent depends upon the whether we take a short-term or a long-term perspective. In the short-term, there are some issues directly concerned with the adolescent's *suicidal* crisis, but in the long-term perspective the suicidal nature of the crisis is much less important. Let us first consider the short-term perspective.

RESPONDING TO A SUICIDAL CRISIS

When we discover that an adolescent is acutely suicidal, there are immediate steps which we ought to take. Obviously, if the adolescent has made a suicide attempt, acute medical treatment must be sought, either through paramedics or at a hospital emergency room. Overdoses, poisons, and wounds must receive immediate medical attention, and most communities have a poison hotline which can suggest important steps to take if the poison ingested is known.

If the adolescent is threatening suicide or seems to have a high risk of making a suicidal act, then emergency psychiatric evaluation and treatment is necessary. Many hospitals and psychiatric clinics have emergency services. Many communities have suicide prevention services (and sometimes teen hotlines) that people can call day or night, seven days a week. These facilities can provide immediate help.

There are several issues associated with this type of emergency treatment. If we come across someone who has made a suicide attempt, we are duty bound to assist them to obtain medical assistance regardless of whether they want it or not. The ethics of intervening with suicidal people are a complex issue (Lester 1981). One guideline for intervention assumes that, if people want to commit suicide, they can usually isolate themselves so that others will not be able to discover them and intervene. If, on the other hand, someone does find them after they have harmed themselves, then the intervener cannot be expected to spend time deciding whether the person has a right to die or not. Interveners ought to initate rescue efforts. The same guidelines would apply to adolescents as well as adults.

With adults, there may be ethical reasons not to force suicidal people into psychiatric care or to call a suicide prevention service. Adults must be considered to be autonomous actors with the right to make decisions about their own lives. They can be advised, but they cannot be coerced. Some psychiatrists (Szasz 1986) are opposed to involuntary treatment of any adult unless they pose a danger to *others*. Other psychiatrists, however, would expand this to include danger to *themselves* or *others*.

In our society adolescents are not usually granted these rights of autonomy. Thus, it is more acceptable for parents to force their children into treatment, even against their will. This *parentalism* is frequently abused, but forced intervention in suicidal crises is probably acceptable. However, the issue of what is the age which makes forced treatment unacceptable remains.

Suicide prevention services are typically staffed by paraprofessionals and usually do not have the power to commit clients for involuntary treatment. They provide crisis counseling which consists of empathic listening to the thoughts and feelings of the client as they discuss their problems, evaluation of the resources of the client, both personal and social, and then suggestions about the steps to take to help resolve the suicidal crisis.

Psychiatric treatment at a hospital or clinic begins with a psychiatric evaluation. This involves assessing the suicidality of the client, with recommendations for hospitalization if the client is considered to be at high risk for suicide, combined perhaps with suicide precautions, including removal of possible methods for committing suicide (such as belts and sharp objects) and placement in special units with continual monitoring.

The second part of a psychiatric evaluation typically involves deciding which psychiatric disorder the client has and, usually, which medication to administer. For example, a diagnosis of schizophrenia may call for a major tranquilizer, whereas a diagnosis of depressive disorder may call for an antidepressant. There are also medications to control a client who is behaving in an uncontrolled manner.

Since this treatment may be forced on the adolescent, great care must be taken in the initial psychiatric evaluation to consider whether hospitalization is appropriate or whether the family can take the adolescent home. Cases in textbooks often present examples of supportive families in whose care the adolescent recovers. In reality, the family is usually part of the problem, and the adolescent will remain in crisis at home. Removing the adolescent from the home, however, requires the involvement of social services, and many communities have social services that are a disgrace to a civilized nation.

All too often, then, those concerned with making the decision as to what to do with the adolescent in an acute suicidal crisis have to choose the best option even if it is not a good option.

LONG-TERM TREATMENT

Once the client is no longer in a suicidal crisis, there is time to explore what are the sources of the adolescent's problems.

What psychiatric and psychological problems does the adolescent have which require treatment? How might these problems best be treated? There are many systems of therapy, and not all may be suitable for every client. A good therapist, therefore, has to choose which system of therapy is best for this client.

Here again, textbooks present a false picture. The textbook writer can describe pharmacological therapy (medications), and the various systems of psychotherapy (including psychoanalysis, cognitive therapy, client-centered therapy, and so on), but the therapist you consult all too often likes only one of these approaches, and that is the one your adolescent gets.

What are the dysfunctional elements in the family which have produced this suicidal crisis, and is the family willing to accept treatment as a unit? Many parents are not willing to accept any responsibility for causing problems in their children. They bring what in their eyes is a defective adolescent for treatment and want the therapist to remedy the defects. Thus, though family therapy may be indicated in some cases, family therapy may be unacceptable to the parents.

The suicidal component of the crisis becomes less important in this long-term perspective. If the adolescent is depressed, then the depression and its sources is treated. If the adolescent is angry, lacks social skills, and is failing academically, these are the issues that are discussed in therapy. If the parents and siblings are part of the problem, family therapy can ease the stress for the adolescent. If the family refuses to consent to family therapy, the adolescent can be helped to survive the family until he or she can escape from it.

Therapy for the adolescent, however, is typically paid for by the parents. Thus, the therapist is an agent for the parents and may not always have the adolescent's interests at heart. Therapists must be careful here. Therapy is not effective if the client does not trust the therapist, and a therapist who abuses the trust ceases to be able to help. We saw in the first chapter how Michael Wechsler's father tried to talk to his son's therapist behind his son's back. We can understand the refusal of Michael's therapist to allow this in the light of the importance of building a sense of trust between the therapist and the client. On the other hand, the father paid the bills!

It must also be admitted here that the various systems of psychotherapy have neglected the problem of suicide. Books which discuss therapy for suicidal clients often trot out a standard discourse on crisis intervention and little else. Most specialized texts on particular systems of psychotherapy do not even mention suicide. For example, I have found no mention of suicide in any works written on gestalt therapy.

To remedy this, Lester (1991) systematically explored how each of the major systems of psychotherapy might view and treat suicidal behavior *per se*, aside from the more general problems which suicidal clients may have.

DISCUSSION

In this chapter we have considered briefly the strategies available for helping the suicidal adolescent. Two final issues are worth noting. First, when an institution or a licensed therapist comes into contact with a suicidal adolescent (or adult) there are clinical and legal standards of care that must be met in order to leave the institution or therapist free from blame for the possible suicide of the client (Bongar 1991). These standards of care are usually in the client's best interests, but they may not always be. They nevertheless must be followed. For example, a therapist with an adolescent who threatens suicide must inform the adolescent's parents.

A second point is that the way in which a therapist approaches a suicidal adolescent may need to be quite different from the way the therapist deals with a suicidal adult. Adolescents generally have very different views from those of adults, may be much more distrustful of the therapist, and may not communicate thoughts and emotions in the same way as adults. Interviewing and conducting psychotherapy with suicidal adolescents requires special techniques and training, and not all therapists may be able to work effectively with suicidal adolescents (Pfeffer 1986; Fremouw et al. 1990).

REFERENCES

Bongar, B. 1991. *The Suicidal Patient: Clinical and Legal Standards of Care*. Washington, DC: American Psychological Association.

Fremouw, W.J., M. de Perczel and T.E. Ellis. 1990. *Suicide Risk: Assessment and Response Guidelines*. New York: Pergamon.

Lester, D. 1981. The morality of counseling the suicidal person. *Journal of Counseling and Psychotherapy* 4(1):79-84.

Lester, D. 1991. *Psychotherapy for Suicidal Clients*. Springfield, IL: Charles C Thomas.

Pfeffer, C.R., 1986. *The Suicidal Child*. New York: Guilford.

Szasz, T. 1986. The case against suicide prevention. *American Psychologist* 41:806-812.

Chapter 13

Helping Your Suicidal Child: A Chapter for Parents

Antoon A. Leenaars, PhD

As we have seen earlier in this volume, both children and adolescents commit suicide. Although suicide is rare in children under the age of 12, it occurs with greater frequency than most people would imagine. The youngest child that I am aware of who committed suicide was 4 years old. Suicide among adolescents occurs with frightening frequency. There is an even greater incidence of *attempted* suicide in children, and the incidence in teenagers is alarming.

An even greater number of our youth contemplate suicide. Pfeffer, in her excellent book, *The Suicidal Child* (1986), reported a study of elementary school children that found that 11.9 percent had suicidal thoughts. In Smith and Crawford's study of high school students, 62.6 percent reported some degree of suicidal ideation (i.e., thoughts of suicide). It is not uncommon for people to have suicidal ideation at one time or another. Be that as it may, this high rate of suicidal thoughts in children and adolescents is of concern to parents and professionals alike.

These facts are, quite understandably, frightening to parents. They are likely to respond, "No one in my family would commit suicide" or "It can't happen to kids." Yet, it does happen—again and again to youths from every type of background and social status. The incidence of self-destructive behavior in teenagers is even more alarming if one includes the large number of single car accidents, their neglect in seeking medical care, the number of cases of anorexia nervosa, and other self-destructive behaviors that often lead to death (Farberow 1980). I remember being asked to see a 16-year-old girl who had a medically diagnosed case of epilepsy for which she had been previously treated. At school, staff were experiencing considerable behavior problems with her. She was also having petit mal seizures. When I talked to her, she stated, "I don't need my pills. I am a big person."

What can we do? What can you, as parents, do? In most cases, something can be done to save a young life. Shneidman (1985) has made a very important observation regarding this concern, namely that about 80 percent of suicides provide clues to their imminent suicide. Regrettably, the clues to suicide are usually not responded to before the act, and sometimes they are not even seen or heard. I have heard very frequently, "I didn't think he'd do it" or "I know she said that she was going to kill herself, but she had said that before." It follows that education about the facts of suicide would help us to prevent suicide. Most people would agree that the best prevention is primary prevention (preventing suicide from ever occurring), and primary prevention involves, among other things, education. It is important to teach which clues should be looked for, what can be done, and what help is available.

As a parent, you are in a unique position to recognize the possibility of suicide and to take preventive action. Parents especially can make a major contribution to saving a life. This chapter is divided into four major sections and a brief concluding remark. The first two sections are on prevention, which, here, relates primarily to dissemination of information. The first part of the discussion offers some important observations from the current literature and the second, some common clues to suicide. The third section is on intervention related to treatment and care of the suicidal person—in other words, what to do. The final major section is on postvention, which refers to those things that can be done for survivors and to how minimize contagion effects.

PREVENTION: SOME OBSERVATIONS

This section consists of eight parts that focus on clarifying suicide in youth: definition, concept of death, facts and fables, depression, learning disabilities, physical disabilities and illness, specific precipitating events and the family system.

Definition

Shneidman (1985) has provided the following definition of suicide: "Currently in the Western world, suicide is a conscious act of self-induced annihilation, best understood as a multidimensional malaise in a needful individual who defines an issue for which suicide is perceived as the best solution."

Pfeffer (1986) suggested that this definition needs to be modified somewhat for youth. She provided the following comment: "It is not necessary for a child to have an understanding of the finality of death but it is necessary to have a concept of death, regardless of how idiosyncratic it may be. Therefore, suicidal behavior in children can be defined as self-destructive behavior that has intent to seriously damage oneself or cause death."

Concept of Death

Do children understand death? Pfeffer's (1986) research suggests that they do, although perception of death differs depending on the age of the child. Young children (approximately at age 7) see death as temporary; everything is seen as alive and vulnerable to death. Children around age 10 see death as personified and temporary and that an outside agent causes death. By the time the child is a young adolescent, say 13, he sees death as final and realizes that internal biological processes cause death. Yet, even older teenagers may sometimes misunderstand the finality of death. For example, Jim, a 16-year-old suicidal individual, was referred to me because of a crisis he was having at home. He wanted to punish his parents and stated, "I'll teach my dad a lesson when I kill myself. Then, he'll learn a lesson." Of course, such reasoning is not logical. Jim could not know what his father's reaction to his death would be. Jim's ideas were based on a denial of what death really means. Teenagers (and adults too) often have an unrealistic concept of death (and also of life). Sometimes, people believe that somehow after they are dead they will actually continue to live in the hereafter. Thus, adolescents have a concept of death but it may be different from an adult's. Incidentally, Pfeffer has shown that intense fantasies about death may be an early warning sign of suicidal risk in youth.

Common Facts and Fables of Suicide

The lore about suicide contains many interesting items. Below we present a number of common fables and facts of suicide, first described by Shneidman. They are facts and fables for all ages.

Fable:	People who talk about suicide don't commit suicide.
Fact:	Of every 10 persons who kill themselves, 8 have given definite advance verbal warnings of their suicidal intentions.
Fable:	Suicide usually happens without warning.
Fact:	Many studies have revealed that the suicidal person gives many clues and warnings

regarding his suicidal intentions. This is not to say that all suicidal people always give warning.

Fable: Suicidal people fully intend to die.

Fact: Most suicidal people are undecided about whether they really want to live or die. Sometimes when they attempt suicide they are "gambling with death," and leave it to others to perhaps save them.

Fable: Once a person is suicidal, he is suicidal forever.

Fact: Individuals who wish to kill themselves are suicidal only for a limited period of time. In other words, it is almost always a temporary state.

Fable: Improvement after a suicidal crisis has occurred means that the suicidal risk is over.

Fact: Most suicides occur within about 3 months following the beginning of "improvement," when the individual has the energy to put his morbid thoughts and feelings into effect.

Fable: Suicide is more common among the rich — or, conversely, it occurs mostly among the poor.

Fact: Suicide is neither the rich man's disease nor the poor man's curse. Suicide is very "democratic" and is represented proportionately among all levels of society.

Fable: Suicide is inherited.

Fact: Suicide does not usually run in families. It is an individual pattern, but it may be a learned behavior, particularly from parents. However, that parents committed suicide does not mean that suicide is genetic.

Fable: All suicidal individuals are mentally ill,
                    and suicide always is the act of a psychotic
                    person.

Fact: Studies of hundreds of suicide notes indi-
                    cate that although the suicidal person is ex-
                    tremely unhappy, he is by no means
                    mentally ill.

In the field of suicide, there are likely to be a number of misconceptions about suicide, including the misconception that when we talk about myths, we understand what people actually believe or know. In order to address this topic, Leenaars and co-workers (1987) administered a questionnaire about suicide derived from Shneidman's facts and fables to a group of Canadian university students, high school students and adults. We found that people's level of knowledge was surprisingly high in all groups; the items answered correctly ranged from 77.5 percent to 84.2 percent. The 100 non-student subjects, many of whom where parents, (mean age of 28 and from two different geographic areas), also had high levels of accurate knowledge. Only two items seemed perplexing to the respondents. Less than 50 percent of all people knew the fact that individuals who wish to kill themselves are suicidal only for a limited period of time and the fact that suicide occurs within about three months following an improvement after a depression. Our results are consistent with a similar study in the United States by McIntosh, Hubbard, and Santos (1985). Similar studies still need to be conducted in other countries to see whether the rather encouraging finding that people are generally well-informed about suicide is true in other countries.

Depression

First and foremost, it must be understood that not all suicidal youths are depressed and that not all depressed youths are suicidal. Depression and suicide are not the same. Pfeffer (1986)

noted, however, that the symptom of depression is one important distinguishing factor between young people who are suicidal and those who are not. Depression can be noted in mood
and behavior (ranging from feelings of dejection and hesitancy
in having social contacts to isolation and serious disturbances
of appetite and sleep) and verbal expression (ranging from
talking about being disappointed, excluded and blamed to
talking of suicide, dying, being abandoned and feeling helpless). Behaviors such as excessive aggressiveness, sleep disturbance, change in school performance, decreased socialization,
somatic complaints, loss of energy, unusual change in appetite
and weight have all been associated with depression (Pfeffer
1986). However, not all depression is noticeable, especially in
young people. Some children, particularly teenagers, show
"masked" depression. For example, anorexia, promiscuity and
drug abuse are behaviors that have been associated with depression. It is important to remember that depression does not
equal suicide in a simple one-to-one fashion. Most suicides
experience unbearable pain, but this pain does not necessarily
show itself as depression (Shneidman 1985). The unbearable
emotion might be hostility, despair, shame, guilt, dependency,
hopelessness or helplessness (Leenaars et al. 1985). What is
critical is that the emotion — pain — is unbearable. Unendurable
psychological pain is the most common stimulus for suicide
(Shneidman 1985).

Learning Disabilities

The importance of brain dysfunction in children and its relation to learning disabilities is well documented. The relation
of brain dysfunction to socioemotional problems is, however,
a more neglected topic in the literature. Peck (1985) observed
that although about 5 percent of the children in the general
population are diagnosed as having a learning disability, in a
sample of suicidal youngsters, 50 percent had been so labeled.
He noted, "it is clear that learning-disabled youngsters may
suffer from loss of esteem and, in those cases where youngsters

experience both pressure from parents to be "normal" and pressure from peers deriding their disability, their feelings of frustration and hurt may be so great as to place a very young child in an at-risk category for suicide" (p. 116).

Rourke and Fisk (1981) documented that different patterns of cerebral dysfunction and their resulting learning disabilities render a child at risk for different types of socioemotional disturbances. They reported three major subgroups. The first group has right brain dysfunction. These children are prone to learning problems with nonverbal and visual information and they also may show the following socioemotional problems: not paying attention to visual objects as well as other people around them; rarely expressing emotions appropriately in their facial expressions; having a voice that can be expressionless; being very talkative; talking to themselves; having flow problems in their speech; and being socially awkward.

The second group has left brain dysfunction. These children are prone to learning problems with verbal information. They may show the following socioemotional problems: rarely initiating conversations; having problems paying attention, for example, in conversation; being withdrawn; being brief and often concrete in their remarks; often responding with the statement "I don't know" to questions; and often being isolated from other children.

The third group has both left and right brain dysfunction and exhibits a combination of the symptoms in the first two groups discussed.

Other more specific cerebral deficits render youth at risk for other specific problems such as planning, or sequencing social events. Although further empirical studies need to be conducted in the neuropsychology of youth suicides, these observations clearly warrant the attention of professionals, parents and teachers. Indeed, Rourke and his associates (1986) have shown that one possible adult outcome of childhood central processing deficiencies is suicidal behavior, as well as other socioemotional problems. Rourke, Young and Leenaars (1987) have suggested that it is especially the first pattern (associated with right brain dysfunction) that predisposes those afflicted to adolescent (and adult) suicide risk.

Physical Disabilities and Illness

I would be remiss if I did not, at least, note the importance of physical problems on the suicidal behavior of some young people. Barraclough (1986) has noted that physical illness interacts with an individual's emotional functioning. Indeed, some illnesses directly affect one's emotions. Some physical illnesses that have been associated with suicidal behavior, according to Barraclough, are anorexia, bulimia, diabetes, epilepsy, traumatic brain injury, and muscular dystrophy. Some people with physical disabilities who are at risk for suicide are those with spinal injuries that have resulted in their becoming quadriplegic or individuals who have had limb amputations. Individuals with HIV virus and AIDS-related syndrome (ARC) also appear to be at high risk (Fryer 1986). I also recall a case of a young male who had a genital deformation and it contributed significantly to his suicidal "solution." However, it is important to realize that not all youths with physical disabilities are suicidal.

Precipitating Environmental Events

A current popular formulation regarding suicide is that suicide is primarily due to an external event; for example, some sort of rejection or perhaps being affected by the music of a pop singer. Despite the fact that precipitating events (deprivation of love, sexual abuse, death of parent, divorce, for example) are frequent occurrences in the lives of most adolescents who have committed suicide, it is less true in young children. Shneidman (1985) has noted that the common trend in suicide is not so much the precipitating event but, rather, life-long coping patterns that the youth has developed. Even in young people one can see patterns of behavior despite developmental changes. Children and adolescents who kill themselves usually experienced a steady toll of threat, stress, failure, challenge, and loss that gradually undermined their adjustment process.

Reflect on the frequent statement "Sally killed herself

because her boyfriend rejected her." Most of us do not commit suicide under such circumstances, so why did Sally? A useful answer to this question is not what kind of person Sally was, but rather what do suicidal youths such as Sally have in common with one another?

One event that has frequently been identified as a possible precipitating event to a child's suicide is the death of their parent (Pfeffer 1986). Indeed, when death occurs by suicide, everyone in the family is at greater risk for suicide since imitation of parental suicide is not uncommon.

This discussion also raises the issue of the contagion (copy-cat) effect. Recently, in Japan, Yukiko Okada, an 18-year-old pop idol, jumped to her death after having a fight with her lover. In the 17 days following her suicide, 33 other young people committed suicide. Phillips (1986) documented that teenage suicide clusters do exist (as discussed in Chapter 8) and that such clustering is more common in teenagers than it is in adults. No research has been undertaken to date on clustering in children. Phillips noted further that when a suicide is sensationalized by the media, there is an increase in the suicide rate, especially for girls. Obviously, this raises the issue of how to expose our youth to information about suicide since we also know that if we do not inform our youth, there will be an increase in suicide rates. Smith and Crawford (1986) showed that suicide is a personal concern for most high school students. Yet, many — especially boys — deny or distance themselves from the problem. It is my belief that professionals, teachers and parents need to work together in developing suicide prevention and postvention programs in their communities and especially in the schools, the latter being especially helpful in addressing the contagion effect (Leenaars 1985, 1986).

Suicidal Youths and their Families

A review of the literature (Corder and Haizlip 1984; Corder Parker and Corder 1974; Maris 1985; Pfeffer 1981a, 1981b, 1986; Seiden 1984; Toolan 1981) suggests that the family system and how it functions is a crucial factor associated with suicide and suicidal behavior in youth, although by no means do all suicidal families show these negative characteristics. There are no universals in youth suicide. However, a few common observations of families of suicidal children are provided as well as a few specific additional observations pertaining to teenagers.

1. There is, at times, a lack of generational boundaries in suicidal families. There is an insufficient separation of the parent from his family of origin. Often grandparents, for example, take over the parenting role.

2. The family system is often inflexible and change of any sort is seen as a threat to the survival of the family. Denial, secretiveness and especially a lack of communication are typically seen in these families. In an attempt to get attention from his father, an 8-year-old boy once reported, "If I try to kill myself, maybe my dad will listen."

    Certain families have stringent discipline patterns and set strict limits on their teenagers, and these rules often impede the teenager in his identity development which is critically important to teenagers. Sometimes, love affairs and other relationships are stopped by parents, and this is often an extremely upsetting interference for teenagers.

3. There may be a symbiotic parent-child relationship. A parent, usually the mother, is too attached to the youth. Not only is such a relation disturbing, but also the parent does not provide the emotional protection and support that a child needs as he grows up. Sometimes the parent treats the child as an adult. One teenager tried to break this bond by attempting to kill herself in her mother's prized car, while another straight-A student intentionally obtained a B, resulting in a parental conflict and a suicide attempt by the youth. Additionally, it has been noted over and over again in children that if a parent dies, the child may kill himself to be magically reunited with that parent.

4. Long-term disorganization (malfunctioning) has also been noted in these families, for example, the absence of a mother or father, a divorce, alcoholism, and mental illness. In teenage girls there is a very high rate of incest, compared to the general population.

In addition, three differentiating observations about the families of suicidal teenagers have been made. First, adolescents in such families often feel a lack of control over their environment. This usually stems from rigid family rules and symbiotic relationships. Second, adolescence is often a time of stress and turmoil. It is not, as some believe, a time of simple joy and peace. Often parents do not allow any conflict, turmoil and development, and when it occurs they interpret the behavior as deviant. Third, recent family disorganizations have been noted in families where there is a suicidal youngster, such as recent moves, unemployment, physical or mental illness or parental conflict.

Berman (1986) has argued that a good deal of the current research has not used necessary control groups; that is, it has not compared suicidal youth and their families with other troubled or non-troubled youth and their families. Thus, the conclusions reached may not really be accurate. It may well be that our information is about families at risk for any kind of perturbation. We may not know how the suicidal family differs from other families with other problems such as promiscuity, drug abuse, delinquency, and learning problems. Be that as it may, we do know that the suicide in young people is very often related to disturbances in the family and, at times, other systems, especially schools (Leenaars 1986).

I also wish to strongly state my opinion that we need to know what suicidal families have in common, as opposed to what kind of parents cause the suicide of their children. There are no evil, weak parents, only perturbed parents or, more accurately, perturbed and suicide-enhancing families.

Prevention: Clues to Suicide

We need to be aware of which behaviors are potentially predictive of suicide. Unfortunately, to date there is no definitive list
of behaviors. Two concepts that may be helpful here are lethality and perturbation. Lethality refers to the probability of a
person killing himself, ranging from mild, to moderate, to high.
Perturbation refers to subjective distress, also ranging from
mild, to moderate, to high. Both lethality and perturbation have
to be evaluated when assessing suicidal risk. It is important to
note that one can be perturbed and not suicidal. Lethality kills,
not perturbation. Perturbation is relatively easy to evaluate;
lethality is not. My own experience with parents, teachers,
clergy and family doctors is that lethality is best assessed by a
professional who is experienced in this area (such as a psychiatrist, psychologist, or social worker). But, it is important that
everyone be aware of these concepts so that they can recognize
the clues the point to potential suicidal behavior. The following
list cites important clues that point to suicidal potentiality.

1. *Previous Attempts*: Although it is obvious that one has
    to *attempt* suicide in order to commit it, it is equally
    clear that the event of attempting suicide need not have
    death as its objective. It is useful to think of the attemp-
    ter, now often referred to as a parasuicide or as a
    self-injurer, and the *completer* as two different parts of
    overlapping populations: one is a group of those who
    attempt suicide, a few whom go on to commit suicide,
    and the other is a group who successfully commits
    suicide, a few of whom may have previously attempted
    to kill themselves. A great deal has to do with the
    lethality of the action. The ratio between suicide at-
    tempts and completions in the general population is
    about 8 to 1 – 1 committed suicide for every 8 attempts.
    However, in teenagers some studies report a rate of 50
    to 1, even 100 to 1. No such data are yet available for
    children.
       A previous attempt is a good clue to the possibility

of future attempts, especially if no assistance is obtained after the first attempt, but not all attempters go on to attempt again (or kill themselves). However, all too frequently such behavior is not taken seriously. I recall a very depressed 11-year-old girl who cut her wrists at school. The principal's response was merely, "She is just trying to get attention." What an extreme way to get attention! The girl was moderately lethal and highly perturbed, and required considerable intervention.

2. *Verbal Statements*: The attitude toward individuals who make verbal threats of suicide is often negative. Suicidal threats are often seen as only attempts to get attention. This attitude results in writing-off and ignoring the behavior of a person who is genuinely perturbed and potentially suicidal. Also, it is a well-documented fact that questioning a person about possible suicidal behavior will not increase the chance that they will commit suicide. The important question is, "Why has this person chosen this particular way of getting attention when there are so many other ways?" Examples of verbal statements from young people follow: "I'm going to kill myself" or "I want to die," are both very direct. More indirect examples are: "I am going to see my (deceased) mother" or "I always knew that I'd die at an early age."

3. *Cognitive Clues*: The single most common state of mind of a suicidal person is known as constriction. There is tunnel vision, in other words a narrowing of the mind's eye. There is a narrowing of the range of perception, opinions or options that occur to the person. The person frequently uses words like "only," "always," "never," and "forever." Examples of this in young people are the following: "No one will ever love me. Only Mom loved me"; "John was the only one who loved me"; "Dad will always be that way"; and "Either I'll kill my brother or myself."

4. *Emotional Clues*: The child or teenager who is suicidal is often highly perturbed. He is disturbed, anxious, and perhaps agitated. Depression, as already noted, is fre-

quently evident. Teenagers are often very angry and hostile and may feel boxed in, rejected, harassed and unsuccessful. A common emotional state in most suicidal people is hopelessness/helplessness. Hopelessness often reveals itself in statements such as: "Nothing will change. It will always be this way." The helplessness can sound like this, "There is nothing I can do. There is nothing my parents can do."

5. *Sudden Behavioral Changes*: Changes in behavior are also good predictors of suicide. Both the outgoing individual who suddenly becomes withdrawn or isolated, and the normally reserved individual who suddenly becomes outgoing and thrill-seeking may be at risk for suicide. Such changes are of particular concern when a precipitating painful event has also occurred. Poor performance in school such as sudden failure may be an important clue. Making final arrangements like giving away a record collection, a favorite watch or other possessions may be ominous and should be recognized as a clear warning sign to parents. Often when this happens, the move is ignored. Perhaps the receiver is too pleased to get the "gift." A sudden preoccupation with death, such as reading and talking about death, may also be a clue. Constructive discussion of this topic as a class project may be helpful for the individual and his classmates since peers are often the first to hear this kind of information.

6. *Life-Threatening Behavior*: I recall a 9-year-old boy who killed himself. He previously had been seen leaning out of an open window of his apartment, and, at another time, playing with a gun. I also know about a 17-year-old teenager who died in a single car accident on an isolated road after having had several similar accidents following his mother's death. Self-destructive behavior is not rare. Often alcoholism, drug addiction, mismanagement of physical disease and auto accidents should be seen for what they might be – suicidal clues. Farberow (1980) has called this, "the many faces of

suicide." Here are a number of questions one should consider: Why did the young child, knowing that the gun was loaded and despite his parents' warnings, play with it? Why did the teenager drive so fast on a slippery wet road when he knew that for the last 3 months his brakes had been bad? Why did a person, knowing the dangers of cocaine use, continue to use it and get hooked? I am not suggesting that these young people intentionally want to die; yet, their behavior made them as "good as dead."

7. *Suicide Notes*: Like prior suicide attempts and verbal statements, suicidal writings that suggest suicidal ideation (as opposed to final suicide notes) are important clues, but, unfortunately, they are often read and ignored by the reader. Such writings are very rare in young children, but more common in adolescents (although most adolescents who kill themselves do not leave a suicide note). Art work, diaries, music, and other personal documents can be seen as similar expressive clues. I remember one suicide note stating, "I finally completed something I've always wanted to do. I removed the guilt from every person... PS: Happy Father's Day."

Below are a number of other genuine suicide notes. They are presented here not merely as a clue but to allow the reader to better understand the subjective frame of mind of our young people who actually kill themselves.

A SAMPLE OF SUICIDE NOTES

1. Single male, age 13:

    I know what I am doing. Annette, I found out. Ask Carol. I love you all.

                                            Bill

2.   Single female, age 16:

> Dear Mother & Dad,
> Please forgive me. I have tried to be good to you both. I love you both very much and wanted to get along with you both. I have tried. I have wanted to go out with you & Dad but I was always afraid to ask for I always felt that the answer would be no. And about Bill, I want to dismiss every idea about him. I don't like any more than a compassion, for a while I thought I did not no more, in fact, I am quite tired of him, as you know, I get tired of everyone after a while.
>   And mother, I wish you hadn't called me a liar, and said I was just like Hap. as I'm not. It is just that I am afraid of you both at times, but I love you both very much.
>
> > So long
> > Your loving daughter
> > That will always
> > love you
> > Mary
>
> P.S. Please forgive me. I want you to, and don't think for one minute that I haven't appreciated everything you've done.

3. Single male, age 18:

> My life would have been a failure anyway. I guess I could have changed, but I just didn't have the will power. I'm sick of suffering and sick of seeing you suffer. Tell _____, Aunt _____ and _____ I love them and am sorry but this is the best way. Return my library books & give my literature books back to school. Demand a refund of $15 tuition & $15 class dues. Bury me in my blue suit & new shoes. Pallbearers _____, _____ and _____. You will find me in the garage.

I would also like to offer one last writing, a suicidal expression, not a suicide note. It was written by an 11-year-old girl (of high perturbation, but low lethality) who was contemplating suicide. She wrote the following to her teacher:

Hi hows your day going? I hope fine. I've been trying hard in french real hard Mrs. T. I know what im going to say isnt your problem but I just needed to tell someone my feelings I can't keep it in. I hate living I want to die noone understands why I cant explain why. I wish I wasn't born why did it hapen to me why did God make me. I'm frightened to get my tests signed even when good ones. I'm scared of failing. No-one really cares any way your a nice friend, special. I hope you have a nice future. The best I really like you and sometimes im afraid to live scared—I want to kill myself but I can't do it cause its against the law. I'll go to the oppisite of heaven. I really like you and want to say your a great friend. I love my family alot also. I love you. Other kids think im a baby writing notes. If it weren't for my stupid eyes I wouldn't be as ugly. I don't understand why im so ugly. I'm not feeling sorry for myself I'm just telling how i feel inside. I don't want to pass cause i want to stay here with you. Sorry if I buged you or took up your time.

  I hate life

P.S. you probably can't read my writing

What is important here is that the teacher responded to the girl. I have other notes where the parents themselves responded. Although not all young people leave notes or show other clues, most do and what is important is that we respond — do something effective!

INTERVENTION: WHAT TO DO

The best thing to do when someone's behavior suggests potential suicide is to show concern, interest and support. Discuss it openly and frankly. Below is a list about what you should do when confronted with suicidal behavior and are concerned about suicidal prevention. It is a guide for parents, teachers, teenagers and others who are concerned. It is derived in part from the superb educational material for students from the Hamilton Board of Education, Hamilton, Ontario, Canada.

What To Do When Confronted with Suicidal Behavior

1. Believe it. Accept the possibility that your child may be in danger. Take it seriously. Do not deny the possibility because children and teenagers do kill themselves.

2. Check it out. You may want to check with your spouse or another adult to see if they share your opinion. Teachers may be a good source of information. Often siblings and even friends know what you are only beginning to believe. You may ask your child directly if he is thinking of killing himself and tell him about the clues you have noticed. Suicidal people are often relieved to find someone willing to talk. Don't be afraid that you are putting the thought in his mind, even with a child.

3. Be calm. Don't panic. It will only increase your child's perturbation and may jeopardize your own ability to act.

4. Listen. Take the time to listen to your son or daughter. Encourage your child to verbalize his feelings and thoughts. Accept what he says without judgment. Don't make false promises that things will get better immediately. Don't allow yourself to be sworn to secrecy.

5. Show that you care. Make it clear to your child that you understand and are really concerned. Let the child know that you care and want to help in a sound supportive fashion. Make yourself available.

6. Get help. Suggest professional help and go with the child for assistance. If he or she refuses help, you should initiate it yourself. Contact a professional. Meanwhile, if the risk of suicide is high, don't leave your child alone. Take the child with you along to a source of help or call a crisis center to assist you with what to do. If the suicidal act is in progress call the ambulance and police immediately. It may be too late

to act later if the child has taken some potential life-threatening action.

The main rule is to get help. Even if you have openly talked with the suicidal youngster, it is a cardinal rule not to take on too much upon yourself. Whenever a serious suicide risk exists, get help from a trained professional through a suicide prevention center, a school guidance office, a mental health clinic, a family physician, a Samaritan center or other appropriate services in your area.

If the youngster refuses help, consult a professional for advice on how to handle the situation. If the youngster, for example, a neighbor's child, your son's friend or even your own child, requests your secrecy, explain and discuss his or her fears but do not swear to secrecy. If it is another person's child, my approach has been to ask "If it was your son, would you want to know?" Most important, don't delay your actions.

POSTVENTION

Postvention is a term originally introduced by Shneidman (1973). It refers to the actions carried out *after* an event has occurred that serve to help the person who has attempted suicide, for example, or to deal with the adverse effects on the survivors (Shneidman 1973).

Postvention includes offering mental health services to the bereaved survivors. It includes service to all survivors who are in need — children, parents, teachers and friends. Shneidman has frequently noted that the further development of suicide postvention services is important. School systems will be a critical force in these efforts with our young people (Leenaars 1985). Parents, too, have a responsibility.

The most important action to take if a suicide occurs in your family is to get professional help for the survivors. Families who do not seek such assistance leave themselves open to a number of "family-destructive" possibilities (such as alcoholism, isolation, divorce, and suicidal behavior). A book for survivors that a number of survivors have suggested to me is Hewett's *After Suicide* (1980).

Suicide postvention in the home is also important. If your son or daughter comes home and tells you about a suicide of a friend or classmate, the first rule is talk about it. Do not walk away and do not ignore it! Although again there is no recipe to follow, there are some suggestions that can be followed:

1. Talk about it: Inquire about what happened. If need be call the school. Discuss the suicide openly and frankly in a supportive fashion.

2. Be calm and do not panic: This response will only increase your child's anxiety. Behave in a quiet, non-sensational fashion.

3. Listen: Take the time to listen. Encourage your child to verbalize his feelings and thoughts.

4. Show that you care.

5. Get help: If you believe that your son or daughter is also at risk for suicide, get professional help — a psychologist, a social worker or other mental health worker.

The purpose of postvention is to deal with your child's reactions to suicide and death, his guilt feelings, his unresolved grief, as well as other reactions. It is not unusual to see reactions such as bad dreams and disturbing thoughts, even months later. A 16-year-old client, who was the next-door neighbor of a young boy who had killed himself, came for help *3 years* after the death.

In the hope of providing a sound model for your child, you should be open about the suicide, without in any way being sensational. Children often know more about suicide than we might assume.

Young people must know that there are alternatives to suicide. Let's say a young woman kills herself after rejection by a boyfriend. Not only must we ameliorate the after-effects of the suicide, but we must help young people to understand that not everyone kills themselves after such an event. Although the young woman may not have seen any alternative, there are indeed other avenues she could have chosen, especially talking to parents and other adults who will talk about problems and listen in a caring fashion.

In postvention it is important to remember that parents are not alone. There are family and community support groups, community supports (and services) available.

A CONCLUDING REMARK

Suicide and suicidal behavior in youth is not uncommon and, although most of us will never experience these events in our own homes, it is important that all of us have a basic understanding of suicide and what to do in critical situations. Your efforts in helping a suicidal person and in making sure that professional help is obtained may very likely save a life. Parents must recognize their role as potential rescuers and can readily learn appropriate ways of dealing with suicidal young people. Parents need to know basic prevention and intervention skills before the tragedy occurs and postvention skills if it occurs. I know of many parents who have used this knowledge to save a life. All of us have a role in this education. The belief that suicide prevention works only temporarily is a myth. With appropriate help, our children and teenagers can be assisted to live long, fulfilling lives.

Acknowledgments

I would like to thank E. Shneidman, C. Pfeffer and the American Association of Suicidology for their education. Many of the ideas in this chapter were gleaned from them. I would like to thank W. Balance and S. Wenckstern for their suggestions and editorial assistance. The cooperation of the Suicide Prevention/Awareness Committee of Windsor in gathering some of the data is appreciated. Grateful acknowledgment is made for permission to reprint the following: "Common Facts and Fables of Suicide" by Edwin Shneidman; excerpts from "Adolescents at Risk: Suicide Prevention" by the Board of Education for the City of Hamilton (Box 558, 100 Main St. W., Hamilton, Ontario L8N 3L1).

REFERENCES

Barraclough, B. 1986. The Relation Between Mental Illness, Physical Illness and Suicide. In J. Morgan, ed., *Suicide: Helping Those at Risk*. London: King's College.

Berman, A. 1986. Suicidal youth. Paper presented at the conference of the American Association of Suicidology, Atlanta.

Corder, B. and T. Haizlip. 1984. Environmental and personality similarities in case histories of suicide and self-poisoning in children under ten. *Suicide and Life-Threatening Behavior* 14:59-66.

Corder, B., P. Parker and R. Corder. 1974. Parental history, family communication and interaction patterns in adolescent suicide. *Family Therapy* 3:285-190.

Farberow, N., ed., 1980. *The Many Faces of Suicide*. New York: McGraw-Hill.

Fryer, J. 1986. AIDS and Suicide. In J. Morgan, ed., *Suicide: Helping Those at Risk*. London: King's College.

Hewett, J. 1980. *After Suicide*. Philadelphia: The Westminster Press.

Leenaars, A. 1985. Suicide postvention in a school system. *Canada's Mental Health* 33(4):29-30.

Leenaars, A. 1986. Suicide prevention in school systems. Workshop presented at the Canadian Psychological Association. Toronto, Ontario, Canada.

Leenaars, A., W. Balance, S. Pellarin, G. Aversano, A. Magli and S. Wenckstern. 1987. Facts and myths of suicide in Canada. Paper presented at the joint conference of the American Association of Suicidology and the International Association for Suicide Prevention, San Francisco.

Leenaars, A., W. Balance, S. Wenckstern and D. Rudzinski. 1985. An empirical investigation of Shneidman's formulations regarding suicide. *Suicide and Life-Threatening Behavior* 15:184-195.

Maris, R. 1985. The adolescent suicide problem. *Suicide and Life-Threatening Behavior* 15:91-109.

McIntosh, J., R. Hubbard and J. Santos. 1985. Suicide facts and myths: A study of prevalence. *Death Studies* 9:267-281.

Peck, M. 1985. Crisis Intervention Treatment with Chronically and Acutely Suicidal Adolescents. In M. Peck, N. Farberow and R. Litman, eds., *Youth Suicide*. New York: Springer.

Pfeffer, C. 1981. Suicidal behavior of children: A review with implications for research and practice. *American Journal of Psychiatry* 138:154-160.

Pfeffer, C. 1981. The family system of suicidal children. *American Journal of Psychotherapy* 35:330-341.

Pfeffer, C. 1986. *The Suicidal Child*. New York: Guilford.

Phillips, D. 1986. Effect of the media. Paper presented at the conference of the American Association of Suicidology, Atlanta.

Rourke, B. and J. Fisk. 1981. Socio-emotional disturbances of learning disabled children: The role of central processing deficits. *Bulletin of the Orthopsychiatry Society* 31:77-88.

Rourke, B., G. Young and A. A. Leenaars. 1987. A childhood learning disability that predisposes those afflicted to adolescent and adult depression and suicide risk. Paper presented at the joint conference of the American Association of Suicidology and the International Association for Suicide Prevention, San Francisco.

Rourke, B., G. Young, J. Strang and D. Russell. 1986. Adult Outcomes of Childhood Central Processing Deficiencies. In I. Grant and K. Adams, eds., *Neuropsychological Assessment of Neuropsychiatric Disorders*. New York: Oxford University Press.

Seiden, R. 1984. *The Youthful Suicide Epidemic*. Public Affairs Report. Los Angeles: Regents of the University of California.

Shneidman, E. Suicide. 1973. In *Encyclopedia Britannica*. Chicago: William Benton.

Shneidman, E. 1985. *Definition of Suicide*. New York: Wiley.

Smith, K. and S. Crawford. 1986. Suicidal behavior among "normal" high school students. *Suicide and Life-Threatening Behavior* 16: 313-325.

Toolan, J. 1981. Depression and suicide in children: An overview. *American Journal of Psychotherapy* 35:311-222.

Chapter 14

Suicide Prevention in Schools

Beginning in the 1980s, elementary schools became more involved in suicide prevention. Students are in school five days a week, for seven or eight hours a day, for nine months each year. Peers, teachers and school counselors are constantly in close contact with students and are, therefore, in an ideal position to notice signs of an impending suicidal crisis and to intervene to prevent it from happening.

Does this close proximity of students to teachers mean that educational institutions should necessarily be involved in suicide prevention? Smith (1991) has suggested issues that he believes provide reasons why schools should be involved. First, schools now do a good deal more than teach students academics; they have added to their pursuits the goals of helping students develop into mature and productive citizens, and this typically includes developing psychological and psychiatric health.

Second, schools try to resolve other problems that interfere with education, such as learning disabilities and obvious psychiatric problems; suicide is certainly a problem that interferes with education. Third, schools have developed resources such as counseling services that are useful for suicide prevention. Fourth, suicide prevention in the schools typically includes an educational component, and so suicide prevention fits in well with the school's health program.

Finally, perhaps the most forceful argument of all, schools have begun to lose the lawsuits that have been brought against them by parents of students who committed suicide. Often, parents feel that if their child has been displaying suicidal behavior at school, then the school should have some responsibility for intervening.

Thus far, there have been three major issues that have emerged in efforts to bring suicide prevention to schools: staff training in suicide prevention, student education in suicide prevention, and the establishment of guidelines and procedures for dealing with the aftermath of a suicide of a student in the school.

SUICIDE AWARENESS TRAINING

Many programs have been established to increase suicide awareness in educators, parents and students. Ryerson (1987), for example, has set up several programs: a 3-hour intensive seminar for educators that covers facts about suicide and techniques of crisis intervention; less intensive programs that cover the same issues for parents; and 4- to 6-hour workshops that provide information on suicide and its prevention for students. The programs also increase awareness of community resources so that students in crisis can be referred for appropriate help.

Spirito and co-workers (1988) trained teachers to provide a 6-week curriculum for students in health classes. The content of the course focused on knowledge, attitudes and behaviors related to suicide, with special attention given to destroying the myths about suicide (such as "Those who talk about it won't do it"). Risk factors and warning signs were reviewed, and students were helped to feel compassion rather than hostility for those in a suicidal crisis. Students were also trained to respond to suicidal peers by using the techniques of active listening (also known as person-centered counseling), providing social support, and trying to get the student to seek help.

PRIMARY PREVENTION

Another area in which schools can work well with students, an area that has been neglected by psychologists and psychiatrists, is primary prevention — in other words, preventing the problem before it starts. Suicide prevention, on the other hand, is based on devising ways of *intervening* once an individual is in a suicidal crisis. It has been hard to devise strategies to prevent people from *becoming* suicidal.

Schools provide an excellent opportunity for primary prevention. Schools could help children develop traits, habits, and skills that would make it less likely that they would ever become suicidal.

To date, school programs have focused primarily on improving the self-esteem of young children, beginning as early as kindergarten (Stivers 1991). Goals have been established (such as providing children with opportunities for experiencing success and independence), and curricula have been devised (Reasoner 1988; Stivers 1991).

POSTVENTION IN SCHOOLS

Our schools need to establish guidelines for teachers on how to deal with students when there is a crisis. Guidelines can facilitate coping with any kind of crisis. Recently, one school experienced the crash of a plane with a helicopter over a playground where many young students were playing. As a result several children were killed and others received severe burns. Mass murders have occurred on school grounds, school buses have crashed causing loss of life, and the disaster of the space shuttle *Challenger* had traumatic consequences for the school staff and children whose teacher was on board. Though perhaps less dramatic, the suicide of a student can also cause a severe crisis for the school, including emotional upset in many of the students and this can even precipitate more suicides (Coleman 1987).

Since community resources are usually required for good postvention, it is necessary to contact community resources *before* any trauma occurs so that coordination and networking arrangements can be worked out. Key agencies must be brought in and community leaders must be involved.

Administrators should have guidelines established for dealing with the news media, especially since the news media can exacerbate a crisis by the way in which they report it. The Centers for Disease Control (1988) have even expressed concern over this issue and have published a set of guidelines. Administrators should also have plans for dealing with distraught parents. An obvious first step would be to designate specific staff members for these tasks.

It would be useful for schools to have staff that are already trained to deal with crises and they should make previous arrangements with local mental health facilities who are willing to provide counselors and consultants for times of crisis, for some students (and staff) may require immediate crisis intervention.

Teachers (and other staff, even including the school bus drivers) should be trained to recognize when a student seems to be in distress. For some students, the distress may not occur immediately after the trauma, but rather it may develop over the next few days or weeks as reality sinks in. Thus, a continuing program lasting several months is important, though of course the level of effort involved should decline over time. A good set of guidelines for postvention in schools has been provided by Wenckstern and Leenaars (1991).

DISCUSSION

The establishment of procedures for dealing with trauma in a school and the introduction of curricula designed to improve the psychological health of children and adolescents cannot be faulted. There has, however, been some criticism of programs to educate students about suicide and suicide prevention. Berman (1991) noted that schools in the United States apparently cannot teach the basic skills of reading, writing and arithmetic very well. How can they be expected to divert resources to teach students about suicide in addition to all of the other social issues that parents demand that schools focus on (such as AIDS, drug abuse and sexual behavior)? The result is that suicide awareness programs are brief one-time workshops, and there is no reason to believe that such brief programs will be effective.

Suicide awareness programs are frequently not evaluated and, when they are, they occasionally (but not always) reveal disturbing conclusions. Shaffer and co-workers (1988) found that the programs they evaluated did not change student attitudes toward the management of suicide, or whether the students would seek counseling if they were in crisis. A small, but significant, percentage of the students at high risk for suicide (for example, those who had attempted suicide in the past) reported that the program had actually increased the difficulties they had in dealing with their problems.

There is a danger too in romanticizing suicide as a possible solution to life's difficulties. For comparison, consider AIDS. Contracting AIDS would not seem to be an attractive goal for anyone. It can be a very dangerous side effect of pleasure-seeking behavior. It should, therefore, be relatively easy to educate people on how to avoid catching it, but this has proven quite difficult (Valdisserri et al. 1988).

In contrast, for those depressed and in crisis, suicide seems to be a viable, even a good choice. Talking about suicide may decrease the fear of death by providing intellectual control over such emotions. Describing cases of suicide, especially those portrayed in videos and television specials for students, may provide role models with whom the suicidal student can identify.

In conclusion, while primary prevention of suicide (and other psychological problems) in school children seems to be an excellent idea and while all schools should have established procedures for dealing with crises, the design and provision of suicide awareness programs, particularly those for the students, requires a great deal more thought and evaluation before we can be comfortable with them.

REFERENCES

Berman, A.L. 1991. Suicide Intervention in Schools. In A.A. Leenaars and S. Wenckstern, eds., *Suicide Prevention in Schools*. New York: Hemisphere.

Centers for Disease Control. 1988. CDC recommendations for a community plan for the prevention and containment of suicidal clusters. *Morbidity and Mortality Weekly Report* 37:5-6.

Coleman, L. 1987. *Suicide Clusters*. Boston: Faber & Faber.

Reasoner, R.W. 1988. *Self-Esteem Curricular Resources*. Santa Cruz, CA: Center for Self-Esteem.

Ryerson, D. 1987. ASAP: An Adolescent Suicide Awareness Programme. In R.F.W. Diekstra and K. Hawton, eds., *Suicide in Adolescence*. Dordrecht, The Netherlands: Martinus Nijhoff.

Shaffer, D., A. Garland, M. Gould, P. Fisher and P. Trautman. 1988. Preventing teenage suicide. *Journal of the American Academy of Child and Adolescent Psychiatry* 27:675-687.

Smith, J. 1991. Suicide intervention in schools. In A.A. Leenaars and S. Wenckstern, eds., *Suicide Prevention in Schools*. New York: Hemisphere.

Spirito, A., J. Overholser, S. Ashworth, J. Morgan and C. Benedict-Drew. 1988. Evaluation of a suicide awareness curriculum for high school students. *Journal of the American Academy of Child and Adolescent Psychiatry* 27:705-711.

Stivers, C. 1991. Promotion of Self-Esteem in the Prevention of Suicide. In A.A. Leenaars and S. Wenckstern, eds., *Suicide Prevention in Schools*. New York: Hemisphere.

Valdisserri, R.O., D. Lyter, L.C. Leviton, C.M. Callahan, L.A. Kingsley, and C.R. Rinaldo. 1988. Variables influencing condom use in a cohort of gay and bisexual men. *American Journal of Public Health* 78:801-805.

Wenckstern, S., and A.A. Leenaars. 1991. Suicide Postvention. In A.A. Leenaars and S. Wenckstern, eds., *Suicide Prevention* in Schools. New York: Hemisphere.

Chapter 15

Coping with the Suicide
of an Adolescent

When a person dies, those close to the deceased typically experience great sorrow, but the precise nature of the emotions experienced probably depends to a degree on the cause of death. A death that is sudden and unexpected may have different consequences for the survivors than a death that was anticipated and for which the survivors had time to prepare. Even with unexpected deaths, the nature of the death may influence the emotional response. Death from murder, for instance, may leave survivors with different emotions than death from suicide or illness.

Death from suicide usually results in a complex and intense set of emotional responses, including sadness, grief, anguish, as well as anger and guilt. Additional emotions are aroused by the stigma that society attaches to suicide. When someone commits suicide, it may suggest that the person had some sort of psychiatric disorder, and this may lead to the suspicion that the whole family is psychiatrically disturbed. If the person who committed suicide was a respected and admired person, friends may wonder if his relatives did something that drove the individual to take his own life.

To explore these issues, research into the aftermath of

suicide has taken two separate approaches. The first method of research has been to question the survivors of a suicide about their reactions, while the second has been to ask members of the general public how they view the survivors of a suicide. The first strategy focuses on the bereavement experience of the survivors of the suicide, while the second strategy focuses on the stigma that the survivors may have to face.

RESEARCH ON THE BEREAVED

Rudestam (1990) pointed out that it is most important to include an appropriate comparison group in studies of the bereaved survivors of a suicide. It is obvious that the survivors of a suicide will experience psychological and physical dysfunctions as part of the grieving process. The crucial question, however, is whether these experiences differ from the grieving process following a nonsuicidal death.

I have already mentioned that a sudden and unexpected death may alter the nature of the grief experienced by the survivors. In addition, suicide may cause certain reactions because the death was violent, guilt because the survivors feel they ought to have somehow intervened and prevented the suicide, and anger at the person for choosing to die in that particular manner. A suicidal death also has an effect on the mourning rituals, such as the funeral and religious services, and may lead to withdrawal of support from social networks because of the discomfort felt by neighbors and friends. Finally, the occurrence of a suicide suggests that the family system may have been dysfunctional, and if this is true, that a particular dysfunctional family may have more difficulty in coming to terms with the death of a family member.

In a novel approach to this issue, Calhoun, Selby and Steelman (1988-1989) asked funeral directors whether they felt that the survivors of a suicide differed from those of a natural death. Two main themes emerged. Family members of a suicide seemed to experience greater shock and more difficulty in dealing with the death, and the suicidal deaths seemed to generate more questioning in the mourners. The funeral directors themselves reported that they felt more constrained in dealing with the family of a suicide and had more difficulty expressing sympathy to them and knowing what to say or do.

In studies of the emotional reactions of the bereaved, Rudestam (1977) has documented reactions of relief, anger and depression in survivors of suicides, but research on people who have lost loved ones to suicide as opposed to other causes have shown that they experience the same emotions with the same frequency (Calhoun, Selby and Selby 1982). Survivors of a suicide, however, seem to experience more of a sense of guilt (Glick, Weiss and Parkes 1974). Cognitive reactions in the survivors of suicide include shock and disbelief, a search for explanations, and denial. Studies that have included a comparison group have indicated that the search for explanations is more intense and less easily resolved if the deceased was a suicide (Sheskin and Wallace 1976).

The precise circumstances of the suicide have been found to affect the resolution of grief reactions. For example, Rudestam (1977) found that the particular family member who actually discovered the dead body of the suicide was slower to recover. The particular way that a person commits suicide can also exacerbate the resolution of grief. A person who shoots himself in the head, thereby disfiguring himself, in a place where he knows that a specific person will discover his body, is obviously expressing anger toward that person.

THE REACTIONS OF THE COMMUNITY TO SUICIDE

Calhoun and his associates (1982) have conducted a number of studies that have explored how people react to suicidal deaths. They found that people viewed the parents of a child more unfavorably if his death was from suicide rather than a virus. The parents of the suicidal child were also viewed as more psychologically disturbed and more responsible for the child's death.

In a later study, Calhoun, Selby and Walton (1985-1986)

extended the focus of the study to include adult deaths. They found that the surviving spouse of a suicide was viewed as more to blame, more likely to feel ashamed of the cause of death, and more able to have prevented the death than the surviving spouse of a person killed in an accident or than a person who died from an illness.

Calhoun, Selby and Abernathy (1986) asked college students what their opinions were regarding social rules for interacting with bereaved persons. There were differences regarding how they felt people should respond to the survivors of a suicide. Saying that the death "was the for best" was viewed as a significantly less appropriate statement for survivors of suicide and accident victims than for victims of leukemia. Similarly, making clear to the survivors that one is aware of the cause of death was also viewed as less appropriate for suicides. These findings suggest that those who could provide support for survivors feel more socially constrained when the death is from suicide. Calhoun found a lack of clarity about what to do for the survivors of a suicide, but greater clarity on what not to do.

These findings are supported by direct interviews with survivors of suicides. Sheskin and Wallace (1976) found that widows of suicides did experience less social support, more loneliness, and more isolation than other widows.

Range and Kastner (1988) found that the stigma surrounding the survivors of a suicide was also present for those close to someone who has attempted suicide. Parents of a psychiatrically hospitalized child were viewed as less psychiatrically disturbed themselves than parents of a child who had attempted suicide. A visit to the parents of a suicide attempter was expected to be more tense. In general, the responses to the family of a child who attempted suicide were identical to those to a family of a child who had died from suicide.

DISCUSSION

In their review of the research, Calhoun, Selby and Selby (1982) noted that no study had yet administered exactly the same interview or questionnaire to comparable groups surviving suicidal deaths versus other types of death. Thus, the conclusions from the research must be regarded as tentative. However, the more intense search among survivors for an understanding of what led up to the suicide and the lower levels of social support that are available to survivors of suicide do seem to be well substantiated.

We might also note that there have been few proposals as to how the survivors of suicides might be helped to resolve both the general and the specific problems they experience. Is there a way public education programs can reduce the social isolation experienced by survivors of suicide? What forms might such education programs take? Attention also needs to be given to those who might interact with the bereaved to ensure that they have an awareness of the special problems facing the survivors of suicide. Goldney, Spence and Moffit (1987) found that, in general, the responses of social workers in Australia to questions about the appropriate social response to suicide were congruent with those of the survivors, while the responses of the general public were often less empathic. The results of this study are encouraging, but efforts need to be made to educate mental health professionals in general on the particular problems faced by survivors of suicide.

In addition, counseling strategies for survivors need to be developed. In recent years, self-help groups for survivors have been set up in many communities, some of which focus specifically on survivors of suicide (Lukas and Seiden 1987), but no exploration of which techniques work best for which clients has appeared to date and no formal evaluation of the effectiveness of these self-help groups has yet been made.

AN INTERVIEW WITH THE MOTHER OF AN
ADOLESCENT SUICIDE

One mother whose 17-year-old son killed himself was willing to let me interview her. Here is the interview in its entirety.

David: What happened to Tim at the time he killed himself?

Jane: He had been away for two days on a camping trip with some friends of his. He was due to come back in the afternoon or early evening of the night that he died. I received a call from my mother-in-law late that afternoon. Tim's father has a country place. Tim and his friends had gone up there and vandalized the place. They had ripped it to pieces; torn up things that would have no real value to anyone but his father. My mother-in-law happened to be going there, and she walked in on them. The boys ran away. She notified the police. Then she became apprehensive and remorseful, and she thought that maybe she shouldn't have notified the police, so she called me. I told her that she was right to do it. Then Tim called me on the way home and I said to him "I talked to Nanny and I know what happened." I worked nights at the time and I said, "If I'm asleep when you get home this evening, you wake me because we are going to talk." He said, "Yes, all right." When I woke up that evening, my other children told me that he had come in, had had something to eat, had said he would be home early and not to bother me. He would talk to me later. He borrowed my foster daughter's car and left. I went to work, but I knew something was wrong. That is the only way I can put it. The idea of suicide never entered my head. Never. But I knew something was radically wrong. I called the police and they told me that they could not look for him until 24 hours had passed. But they said if Lillian, my foster daughter, would declare her car stolen then they could look for him. I called her up and told her to do this. She said she wouldn't. They have a very close and loving relationship. She said there was a reason. Maybe he'd had a flat or something. She wouldn't call the police. I said, "You've got to." She finally gave in and called them. She had an apartment adjoining mine at that time, in a rural area with lots of trees, and there was a parking area. She had a souped-up car. It had decals and flags and everything. So the police came to the apartment to interview her. This was about one o'clock in the morning. She described her car and they said, "Well, that car is in the parking lot." She said, "It can't be, because whenever he returns my car he brings me the keys." The policeman told her the car was in the lot. And she said, "Something is wrong." She went outside with them and they found him. He had taken a piece of garden hose and had threaded it from the exhaust through the window.

David: How old was Tim?

Jane: He was 17.

David: And you say that the thought that he was going to kill himself never entered your mind?

Jane: Never.

David: He never talked about suicide?

Jane: Never to me. But I found out later that to several of his friends and his older brother, he had said that he had considered it (these were not his exact words, of course), that suicide was the ultimate answer, that if

	things got to where he absolutely couldn't handle them, then he'd get out of it. It was the ultimate running away because nobody could bring you back.
David:	But he never mentioned that he had thought of killing himself to you?
Jane:	No, never.
David:	And he had never made any suicidal attempts before?
Jane:	Never.
David:	Did he leave any note?
Jane:	Nothing.
David:	Where did he get the garden hose from?
Jane:	Well, we had a garden hose.
David:	He got that from the house and then he came over to borrow the car?
Jane:	Yes. Apparently he had gone out for a while. I understand he did go over to see his girlfriend for a little bit. But he had come back.
David:	Did you find out whether he had mentioned his intention to his girlfriend?
Jane:	No. She was totally stunned.
David:	He was with some friends at the cabin. Did you talk to them at all?
Jane:	No. They weren't coming near me. All of his friends rallied round. I had an extra 15 children. But those two never came near me. I can understand that.
David:	So it really came as a surprise to most people?

Jane: Yes.

David: Maybe you could tell me something about what Tim was like as a child?

Jane: Well up to the age of about 11, he was a super-sweet child, very sweet, very loving. Totally dominated by his older brother. His older brother led him around by the nose.

David: How much older was he?

Jane: Two and a half years. He really lead him around by the nose. They were like the chief and the indian. Everybody adored him, and he was just sweet and lovable, a little chubby cute kid. Then when he was about 11 he shifted into high gear. He started getting into all kinds of trouble at school. But it was nothing but silly trouble, cutting up, silly trouble. Then we moved up north. I think he was about 11. And then he started really getting into trouble. He set a couple of fires, he vandalized quite a bit, and he began to steal. When I would ask "Why? Now just tell me why," he would say, "I don't know." And I honestly believe he was telling the truth.

David: This all started just before you moved and then it got worse?

Jane: Yes.

David: Is there anything that happened around that time?

Jane: No. We loved it up north.

David: Did Tim have any younger brothers or sisters?

Jane: Yes. He is the middle of 7 children.

David: So there would have been a succession of
            children being born?

Jane: Yes. And they were right close together, all
            of them. There were 7 in 9 years. They're
            are all exceptionally close, including him.
            The times those kids lied for him!

David: So, all his brother and sisters were born by
            the time he was 12?

Jane: Yes.

David: You mentioned a foster daughter. You had
            foster children?

Jane: No. That is just a term we used. She was
            grown when she came to live with us. She
            was a co-worker of mine. She was in her
            early 20s. She had come from New York
            and had been staying with her sister, but it
            wasn't working out. She missed her parents
            and yet she liked it down here. So I said,
            "Come and stay with us." She wound up
            staying for several years and then she got
            her own apartment right next us. She is in
            her late 20s now. I have a little cottage and
            she lives right next to us. The children al-
            ways introduce her as their sister.

David: It's a very close friendship?

Jane: They were close to each other. She had a lot
            of emotional problems, and I think that's one
            reason that they understood each other.

David: So at the age of 11 he started changing.
            What did he do before you moved?

Jane: Well it was just silliness. Like the teacher
            would go out of the room and come back
            and find him tap dancing on a desk. Stick-
            ing bubble gum where bubble gum didn't

	belong. Silly childish things. Like "Look at me. I'm going to make you laugh. I'm a clown."
David:	But it was kidding around?
Jane:	Yes. It wasn't any real harm. It was a nuisance more than anything else.
David:	Then after you moved it began to get bad. What did he set fire to?
Jane:	Once, there was some type of entertainment going on at school. He went to it with a bunch of others, and they went outside during an intermission. He lit a spill or something and tossed it under a parked school bus. Apparently somebody managed to put it out just before it was going to take the gas tank up. He had no idea what would have happened. He was just being stupid. Another time, he set a fire in a classroom. They were making something with rubber cement, and the teacher left the room for a minute. He set fire to that. He swore on a stack of Bibles he didn't do it. But he did. Then another time, riding home from school on the school bus, he and another kid just carved up the whole back seat. Of course, we got the bill for that, which was only right.
David:	So most of his destruction was to objects outside the home. Did he destroy things at home?
Jane:	Not unless he was putting his brothers through the wall. He made rather large holes in the wall.
David:	But usually it was external problems outside of the home?

Jane: Yes.

David: So the night that he killed himself, when he had been up at that cabin and he had taken that apart, was that the first time he had destroyed something that belonged to a relative?

Jane: He did one other thing to a relative. My brother had a coin collection. It was a big bottle, a liquor bottle, and it stood about this high and he kept coins in it. Tim appropriated that. But when it was discovered that Tim had taken it, he paid it all back. That was the only time a relative was involved. He got caught all the time doing things to other people. Once, just before Tim died, the father of a girlfriend was redoing her bedroom, and he had been putting aside money a little at a time so that he had about $1000 on hand. He was taking the money and buying the things that he needed for his daughter's bedroom. She told Tim how pretty her room was. I don't remember whether she took him in and showed him or whether she told him. But at any rate, her father kept the money in a desk. Tim went in there (this was just a day or so before he died), pried open the desk, but took nothing out of it, and then he went out the window. They know it was him because, if you please, he left his knife with his initials on it. He wasn't stupid. He had to be trying to say something. We tried so hard to find out what it was that he was trying to say and we failed.

David: Did he steal from shops?

Jane: He stole anything from anybody, everywhere. You couldn't sit your purse down.

	You couldn't sit your billfold down. You couldn't sit your cigarette case down.
David:	Did he steal money?
Jane:	Yes.
David:	Did he steal things that he needed or just anything?
Jane:	It was anything. For example, I was doing some work in the house with some wood. I was carving this piece of wood and he said, "You are going to tear your hands up with that. I'm going to see if I can find you something that would be better." A day or two later he brought me this wood-working tool, which was really nice. I just said, "Thanks." If I had thought about it, I would have thought he had bought it. He had jobs here and there. He earned money and he was generous. I never even thought about it. It turned out he had lifted it from school. So when this was brought to my attention I shook down his bedroom and pulled the other things out and we took it back to school, I said to him, "Why?" He said, "Well, I thought you could use it." I said, "If I wanted one bad enough, I would go out and buy it. It was nice to have, but not to the extent that I wanted you steal it. If I wanted it bad enough, I could have scared up five dollars and got it."
David:	So he stole generally to give to other people too?
Jane:	Yes, and he stole for himself.
David:	Did he have enough money that he didn't have to steal if he needed those things?
Jane:	Oh yes. He always had jobs. He did beauti-

ful wood work, he did gardening. Anything he turned his hand to he did well.

David: Were there any other behavior problems he showed beside stealing and vandalism?

Jane: A great deal of violence. He had immense mood swings. They were like that [She snapped her fingers]. They swung one way and they swung the other, and when he was in a rage you had just better get out of the way. He would lay you out. He didn't care who you were or what the situation was. He thought the world of his younger brothers, but he still put them through the wall and really let them have it.

David: Can you identify the kinds of situations that would make him angry?

Jane: Anything. Here's one example. His older brother was using my car for some errands, and he parked where he wasn't supposed to park. The policeman asked him for the registration and license. So he pulled out the registration I had in the glove compartment and went into his billfold for his license. It wasn't there. Luckily the policeman was nice enough to accept his word and didn't make any fuss. But my son was really upset. He said to me, "I really don't know where that license went. I know it was in my billfold, and I'm really upset. I could have been taken off to jail." Which was true because he was a long-haired kid. We had a shake down all over the place. We asked Tim, but he said he didn't have any idea where it was. One of my younger sons said to me, "I bet I can tell you where it is." I said, "Where?" "Go under Tim's mattress." We looked and there it was. He had been using it. He was a big, good-looking kid, and had been using it for proof of age to go into bars and get drinks. I talked to him. I didn't always talk to him quietly. I talked at the top of my lungs half the time. But this time I talked to him quietly. I said, "You know this is really something else. It's not only an illegal thing you are doing, but it is a pretty darn rotten thing you're doing. Your brother could have been carted off to jail." He said, "I know," and he double-talked his brains out. Finally I turned him loose. Before I had my back turned on him, Tim threw his brother right through the wall for telling on him. There was a hole in the sheetrock.

David: You said his moods would swing. What other moods did he show?

Jane: I have a hair-trigger temper myself. We would be yelling at each other, and in the middle of things (he would be cussing me up, down and sideways), in mid yell, he would say, "Mom. I love you. I love you." In mid yell. I honestly don't think he knew why any more than the rest of us. There were times when I was so desperate I said to him, "You tell me what you want and I will get it for you. I don't care what it is. I don't care if I have to buy it. I don't care if I have to take another job to get it. I don't care if I have to bribe a politician. You tell me what you want and I will get it for you." He couldn't tell me.

David: Did he show much depression in his teen-age years?

Jane: No.

David: He was relatively happy?

Jane: No. I can't say he was happy. He was usually on a rampage somewhere.

David: What do you mean by that?

Jane: He was an excellent driver but, when he got in a mood, he drove like a idiot. He would get into fights for no reasons. Not just at home, anywhere.

David: So what would he do on a typical weekend or in the evenings? What were his interests?

Jane: Breaking in some place.

David: Did he have a social group that he hung out with?

Jane: Oh yes. They were odd. They were spooky. They disappeared in and out of the woodwork. They were odd. There were a couple of nice straight-forward kids, but they didn't last long as friends.

David: Do you think that his friends were similar to him? Did they break and enter too?

Jane: Oh yes. A lot of them have been in a lot worse trouble since Tim went. We were all hoping that, maybe as ghastly as his situation was, it might bring somebody up short. But it didn't. Just for a little while. All these kids turned up at his funeral, except the two he was with at the cabin. They were all at his funeral, these hoods, all dressed up. They were starched and combed. It would break your heart. They all came up to me and I thought, "Come on. Think. Don't forget this. Think about this. Look at that coffin. Look at it." You wanted to shake them and say, "Look at it. There but for the grace of God." I think it straightened them out for about 4 or 5 days. Like a heavy smoker always says, "The other guy will get lung cancer." I don't think they could conceive of it happening to them.

David: Looking back, do you see his behavior a result of the crowd he was with?

Jane: I can't say that. I never have been one to believe that he led her astray, she led him astray, they led them astray. I figure if you're going to do something, you are going to do it. If you don't want to do it, you're not going to do it. You will find people to do this or that with you if you want company, whether it breaking and entering or sitting and reading the Bible.

David: So you feel that he chose those friends as his friends because they were the ones like him. Was he ever violent toward you?

Jane: Oh yes. He chipped the bone in my wrist one time. I can't remember what the situation was about. It must have been fairly trivial or I would remember. But it degenerated into a battle of wills. I said, "You will." He said, "I won't." He wound up letting my wrist have it. He was totally devastated.

David: In a situation like that, as soon as he hurt your wrist, would that end the emotion?

Jane: Yes. He was horrified.

David: Was he violent toward his father too?

Jane: No. He was 12 when my husband and I separated.

David: So he hadn't been violent up to that point?

Jane: Well, yes. But he knew he couldn't lick his

	father. The time would have come when he would have been able to. If we had been living with his father at the time he died, he and his father would have had it out over the tables and over the chairs. I know it. But at the time there wasn't much he could do about it if his father chose to lay him out.
David:	Did he and his father see each other?
Jane:	Once in a while. He had planned to stay with his father one time. His father was remarried by then. To a much younger girl. Tim liked her very much. One of the reasons he and his father tangled was because Tim objected to his father's treatment of his wife. She is a very tiny little thing, and they were all out raking. He said his father was barking out orders at Susan like a sergeant. I asked, "Was he rude to her?" He said, "No. He wasn't rude. He was speaking very affectionately, but he was saying pick this up, lay that down, shift that here. You know what a peanut she is. Finally I took the rake out of her hand, spun her around by the shoulders, shoved her in the house, closed the door, picked up the rake and continued to work." I asked, "What did Daddy say." He said, "Daddy asked me what I thought I was doing. I said, in case it slipped your mind, that's your wife, not a pack mule." They had a verbal argument over that.
David:	Was his father a violent person?
Jane:	He could be.
David:	When he punished the children, did he beat them or hit them?
Jane:	It depended on which child. He had favorites, and Tim was an unfavorite. My hus-

band is a fantastically brilliant person. Very
brilliant and very creative. One thing where
he was like Tim is the mood swings. Ter-
rific mood swings. He was usually on top
of the world or down in the dumps. First,
there was this project and then there was
that project. Everyone was expected to fall
in with the enthusiasms and drop them
when he did. It was difficult to follow him
at times.

David: You said Tim wasn't one of his favorites.
Was Tim a special target?

Jane: Yes, he was.

David: Can you give me an example of how his father picked on him?

Jane: Tim was supposed to be stupid and clumsy.
All kids are stupid and clumsy at times.
When my older son and Tim and his father
were doing something together, Tim was
the gopher. When he was younger he loved
it. "I am helping Daddy." But then he got to
realize that he wasn't doing any of the fun
parts, and it bothered him.

David: It sounds as though his father might have
put him down verbally?

Jane: Oh yes. A lot. But I can't point to that, because there are so many people who have
bad relationships with a parent, and come
out fine. You just can't say, "His father
picked on him, therefore."

David: Did his father didn't show the episodes of
violence that Tim showed? Losing his temper? Getting into a rage?

Jane: Not to that extent. Not for small reasons.
He had a violent temper. But usually you

knew what triggered him off. With Tim you didn't know what triggered him off. Just a few days before he died (I didn't learn this 'til much later) Tim was working on Lillian's car. (That was the car that he died in.) He was doing something to it and he needed a tool. He went over to my brother's house to borrow it. So my brother was helping him work on the car. Tim said, apropos of absolutely nothing (they weren't talking about anything personal, just what was the matter with the car), "I can't tell you how I despise myself." My brother said, "Why?" He said, "Because everybody forgives me. Everybody gives me chance after chance, and I spit on them. Whenever I do something stupid, Mom screams, yells, throws a tantrum, bounces things off the wall, and then she pulls herself together and gets me out of it. She helps me. She's only one. Dozens of people have done it. And I spit on them, and I don't know why." Then he started to talk about cars. My brother told me that quite some time after Tim died. So apparently the idea of suicide was germinating for some time.

David: Was there anybody that Tim wouldn't act violent toward?

Jane: My mother. That's about it.

David: What about Lillian?

Jane: No. He never would. He nicknamed her the Puerto Rican cannon ball, because one night he got arrested. (One of the many times.) He called her house instead of mine. (I wasn't home anyway. I was working.) She drove out to where he was to get him out of jail. He claimed it was for loiter-

ing, but I think there was a little more to it
than that. I never did hear, because that
was shortly before he died. But she came
out and got him. He said they had him
handcuffed to a bench. Now, like I say, I
think there was more to it than loitering, because you don't handcuff a vagrant to a
bench. Lillian is a very quiet, very gentle
girl. She never raises her voice. He said she
blew into that police station like a Puerto
Rican cannon ball. She flew up to him,
grabbed him and said, "What have they
done to you? You get a key and you get him
out of here!" She ripped the whole station
apart. He said that that was the only time
he had ever seen her lose control of herself.
She's very quiet, repressed, too repressed.
They got along great.

David: Was he violent toward his sisters as well as
            his brothers?

Jane: He had been on occasion. The girls spoiled
            him rotten. When they did come down on
            him, which was not very often, he would
            back off.

David: Before that last time you saw him, before
            he took off for the cabin, or a couple of
            days before, can you remember what he
            was like?

Jane: He told me he wanted to go away for a cou-
            ple of days with his friends. I said, "Sure,"
            and I think I gave him a few dollars, what I
            had. Then I packed up a bunch of food I
            had. All the kids liked canned stew. I gave
            him several cans of that, and what else I
            could spare. He had a sleeping bag and a
            few things. I said, "Give me a call," and he

	said, "OK," and that was the last time I saw him.
David:	Did he seem in his usual mood?
Jane:	Yes. He said to me, "We might stop by and see Dad." So I don't think they had planned on the vandalism, because he wouldn't have told me where he was going. Despite all his times his father called him stupid, he was plenty smart. He took his senior year in high school in 3 months and graduated at age 16. He crammed with a learning center because he was bored. He didn't like school. So I said, "You get your diploma and I will get off your back."
David:	In the days before he went off for the trip, there was nothing to indicate to you that things were getting worse for him? They weren't getting worse or better as far as you could see?
Jane:	No. There wasn't anything to put your finger on. Of course, everybody has a good case of hindsight. We are all very good at that. You think of all these little things. He did beautiful wood work, and anything around the house. If I wanted something done, I asked him, and he would do a beautiful job, always. I bought some tile for the floor and it had to be set a certain way to make the pattern come out right. He was going to put it down, and he just hadn't gotten around to it. He would have, very definitely. He hadn't gotten around to it. He always used to say he was going to see the world. He wanted to go around the world and come home and stick with me and take care of me. I said, "Yes, if I let you grow up. I may head for Tanganyika myself." It was

like a joke between us. So he was off somewhere, one afternoon, and my younger son
(who was at that time about 11) said to me,
"I want to lay the tile." I hated to tell him
no, but I spent some money on that stuff. I
said to him, "I will let you start, but if you
make one mistake you're going to have to
stop, because I paid too much money for
this." He said, "That's fair." He started laying. He was going great guns and doing an
absolutely beautiful job. We hear Tim outside, and he said, "Oh boy. I'm going to
have Tim look at this." So he ran out and
he grabbed Tim. He said, "Come and see
what I did; come and see what I did." So
Tim said, "Hey. You've been laying the tile."
The younger one, Joe, he said, "You check it
out, Tim. You look it over carefully because
Mom wants it done right. It's important to
her. She paid a lot for it." He got down on
one knee and looked along the seams, and
he really hammed it up. Finally, Tim got up
and he said, "That's beautiful. You couldn't
have done better. It's a really good thing, because Mom will always have you to help
her." That was the first time he had ever
given any indication that anybody other
than himself was going to be the one helping me later on.

David: And looking back on that...

Jane: I just thought it was very cute that he ca-
              tered to the little one's desire to be praised
              and so forth. I thought that was cute. But,
              looking back on it, I get a big case of hind-
              sight.

David: Were there any more episodes like that, because you mentioned a conversation you had with his older brother.

Jane: Well the only one I can think of was actually that night that he died. I was still asleep, and he told the kids not to wake me up, that he would talk to me later. My younger son told me this. It had been my birthday that day before. He was away camping. All the kids gave me a little surprise party. They made a cake and gave me presents. Tim wasn't there. Tim was always the one that got something special for me. They all gave me nice presents, but he always made kind of a thing of it. He would make something or build something. He did such beautiful wood work. My younger son told me, "Tim came in and heated up the macaroni. I made a big pot of macaroni that was in the refrigerator. So he took some macaroni and he heated it. I sat down and I was talking to him. He was telling me about camping." I guess he deleted quite a bit. I said to him, "Tim, you should have been here last night. You missed a lot of fun." Tim said, "I did. Why? What happened?" My younger son then said to Tim, "We gave Mom a party for her birthday and it was really nice. Tim looked at me and he said, 'Oh wow. Her birthday.' He finished eating and he went out and asked Lillian for the car." Now I don't think he killed himself because he forgot my birthday. But he had never forgotten my birthday. I mean, nothing was preventing him from going out and getting something later. But it is just all these things. As I said to the kids then, when I had to come back from the hospital and tell them that he was a dead on arrival there,

they all said, "Why didn't I do this, and
why didn't I do that?" And I said, "Company halt. Let's stop right here. No one is al-
lowed to 'if,' because it is the stupidest
word in the English language. No one is al-
lowed to 'if.' If anyone was going to 'if,' I
should. I am his mother. No one is going to
do it." I honestly think the reason he killed
himself (I believed it then, I told the kids
then, and I believe it now) was that he just
said to himself in effect, "I can't stop whatever this is that is driving me. I'm hurting
people. I'm going to hurt them worse. I am
going to stop." I honestly think that's how
it was. I really do.

David: And nobody was to blame?

Jane: Oh, definitely. If anything, I was, as his
            mother. Those kids were so good to him.
            They really were. Too good in lots of ways.

David: What was the effect of his suicide on the
            family? Did it have an effect?

Jane: I don't think it made any changes, other
            than — this is going to sound absolutely
            horrible. Horrible as we all felt, much as we
            missed him and the terrific load of guilt
            that we were all under (in spite of the fact
            that we realized intellectually that we
            weren't guilty; emotionally you will never
            feel that you are not guilty), it was almost a
            relief. For years, every time the phone rang
            or I heard a siren, I would lose my stom-
            ach. Ask not for whom the bell tolls. I gen-
            erally was right. It was the police coming to
            our house. Or the police were on the
            phone. It took me a good year after his
            death to stop reacting like this to a police
            siren or a telephone call. I remember being

out in a car just a few days after he died and hearing a police siren. After my initial reaction, I said to myself, "All right. You're safe now. You're safe." I must say that I have absolutely nothing but praise for the police. They gave that kid so many chances. I could never holler about police brutality. Never. They were so good and so understanding. Too much in some ways. I said, "Listen. Take him out in the back lot and work him over if you feel like it." Really fantastic. But I still had that feeling that he was safe. I think we all did.

David: You are talking as if Tim was the problem child out of the 7.

Jane: He was.

David: The other children never showed...

Jane: No. I got a couple of pains, but no.

David: When psychologists write about families, they often say sometimes there is one person who...

Jane: Is a scapegoat?

David: Right. When that person no longer is there, then somebody else becomes the scapegoat. That hasn't happened?

Jane: No. I do not like their life styles, but they have done nothing that hurts anybody. They're their own worst enemies. As far as my relationship with them, they have always been perfect. I really don't know.

David: Did you ever have any theory about why Tim developed this way? It is as if it was some compulsion that he couldn't control. It started around age 11. Did you ever think

	that there was something physiologically wrong?
Jane:	I hoped there was. Really. That sounds like a stupid thing say. But it would lift such a load of guilt. My husband, their father, has radiation sickness. He told me a couple of years ago, when he knew he was developing symptoms, he said to me, "I have been reading up on this. There isn't a heck of a lot I haven't read about this. I read that the children of people with this (apparently it's cumulative, and he has been working with this since he was 18, since he was in college) they are very prone to certain types of physical diseases. First of all, it's more men than women, more boys than girls. They have a lot of urogenital problems, prostate problems and so forth. Much more than the average person. They are much more prone to psychological and psychotic reactions." I said, "If I could believe that (I know this sounds absolutely horrible) but if I could say this was something that we couldn't help, oh that would be like..." But of course you can't. You can't. That's just too easy. That's too big of a cop-out.
David:	And yet it sounded as if there is not much that you could have done differently.
Jane:	Precisely. I could have tried to hold my temper a little more. But looking back on it, I would just reach a point where I would be so devastated that I think if somebody had held a gun to my head and said, "Shut up!" I couldn't have.
David:	Did Tim ever show any other symptoms beside the behavioral problems? Did he show any abnormal, strong fears?

Jane: No.

David: Was he a bed-wetter?

Jane: No.

David: Any other kinds of symptoms of emotional
             problems? You mentioned before that you
             had made some attempts to try and get
             some help for him. What kind of things had
             you tried?

Jane: We took him to a psychiatrist, and the psy-
             chiatrist gave him tests (he had to draw a
             person, a house and so forth). Tim told me
             he took to him right off. He was supposed
             to be the best for adolescents in mucho
             miles around. The doctor told me that Tim
             showed low self-image, but didn't show de-
             structiveness or anything. Of course, this
             was about 3 years before he died. I'm very
             bad about time. Three years, I guess, be-
             cause it's 4 years this week that he died.
             The doctor talked to him, and he worked
             with him a little. He said to me, "You are
             going to have a fantastic man here." I said,
             "Am I? If I live through this." He said if we
             could just kind of bear with him, we would
             have a fine man. The doctor also said, "I re-
             ally don't think he needs counseling." Then
             I took him for months and months to a
             children's psychiatric center, which is
             good. Then we also had counseling through
             the school. As far as that was concerned,
             we might as well as have saved our breath
             to cool our porridge.

David: How did he respond? Was it usually your
             idea to seek out a counselor?

Jane: I would suggest it, and he would go right
             along. "Yes. If you think so Mom. If you'd

like to, OK." In fact, at the children's psychiatric center, he paid for it.

David: He paid for it?

Jane: Out of money that he earned. After a certain point he said, "Mom, this is stupid." I said, "You're right. This is stupid." We just weren't getting anywhere. This sounds like I'm pointing the finger, but it's not so. I don't blame anybody. I am his mother and I couldn't do anything. Nothing helped.

David: And he felt he wasn't getting anything out of counseling?

Jane: Right. The one who he really responded to was the psychiatrist, and the psychiatrist said he didn't really think he needed day-to-day or week-to-week counseling. So that was the end of that.

David: So Tim himself was never resistant to the idea of therapy? You said that sometimes, early on, he would deny that he had done particular things?

Jane: Always. Look you right in the eye and lie.

David: Were there times when he would sit down and admit that he had done these things?

Jane: Only when he was totally pinned to the wall, when his finger prints and his shoe prints and his coat with his name on it were there. But not one split second before.

David: And then, would he admit it that he had a problem, that he needed help?

Jane: Not really. Just that he didn't know why. Or he would have some totally ignorant reason. Like the time he got that wood chisel

	for me. "You were messing up your hands with the one you were using."
David:	The problem is that teenagers in general are not the kind of people who would sit down and talk about their problems. Most teenagers are not that reflective about their behavior, at least not on the outside.
Jane:	Especially not to somebody of another generation.
David:	Right. So one wouldn't really expect him to sit down and say, "Look I have this problem."
Jane:	No. In most cases, no. Of course it does happen sometimes.
David:	I would think that teenagers are perhaps the most difficult kind of people to help.
Jane:	I would imagine so.
David:	Was there anybody that he had talked to more? Like Lillian or one of his brothers or sisters? Or was he isolated from all of them?
Jane:	I don't think any of them really saw in him a complete person, including myself. I don't think they did. Some saw a better side of him then others did.
David:	After somebody kills themselves, often the members of the family feel some stigma, as if the neighbors are looking at them strangely...
Jane:	No, no!
David:	You never felt that?
Jane:	No, never! We were never allowed to feel that way. There were just too many loving people.

David: So you got a lot of support from other peo-
              ple?

Jane: Everywhere.

David: And you yourself have been willing today
              to come and talk to me.

Jane: How is our time here? I want to tell a little
              something that will digress, that will give
              you an idea. I am a nurse, and I believe
              very definitely in organ transplants. I
              wished a million times that something
              could have been salvaged from Tim. But of
              course there wasn't. He was a DOA. I
              wished so many times there was something
              that would have made it less senseless.
              About a year and a half ago, my sister, who
              is much younger than I am (she is the age
              of my oldest daughter) she and her hus-
              band lost their young child. A congenital
              heart problem, kidney, everything was
              wrong. He died following open heart sur-
              gery. When they knew there was no hope,
              just a day or so before he died, they said,
              "Where do we sign? If there is anything that
              you can take from him, if there is anything
              you can do (we know you can't save him)
              that will help others, do it. Don't tell us
              about it. Just where do we sign?" So he
              died, and a matter of hours after he died
              my sister was on the phone to me. I was
              crying my eyes out. She was on what I can
              describe only as a high. She was euphoric.
              She said to me, "Guess what?" I said,
              "What?" She said, "Dr. Smith said to me
              that they couldn't use any of John's organs
              because there was too much damage. But
              he told me that, because of what they
              learned from John, they will save the next

one. Guaranteed! The next one will live
and be well. Isn't that fantastic?" Well, I
was crying my brains out. I said, "Does it
sound stupid to say I envy you?" She said,
"No never. Never, never, never, does it
sound stupid for you to say that." Now to
me, this type of thing, this is my organ
transplant. This is my autopsy. This is
something to make it a little less senseless.
If it touches one person who can help another person, one that's all. That's all right.

David: To help alert people to the problems and to
sensitize them. That's a nice idea. Specifically, if you think back, is there anything
you could advise or tell a parent who has a
child that's a problem? What should they
do or what shouldn't they do?

Jane: No.

David: You said that maybe if you could have held
your temper back...

Jane: No. I really don't. I can't give one tiniest bit
of advice. Not one. I say, "I should have
held my temper," because we should all
hold our temper. There were many times
when I did hold my temper. When I said,
"Now you tell me. Ask and it shall be
given. I'll do it. I'll get it. I'll buy it. I'll obtain it. I'll arrange it. Whatever will take
this compulsion away from you. If you
want to go around the world on a tramp
steamer, I'll find you a ticket. Anything." I
did hold my temper, but I accomplished
just as little as when I screamed, yelled,
and bounced things off the wall.

David: After all, you acted yourself with your
other children.

Jane: Yes. They got things bounced off the wall a
                   few times too.

David: Right. It really is a difficult problem to
                   know how to deal with the adolescent.

Jane: It is that. Right now, I have two boys at
                   home. They are 15 and 17. One is in high
                   school and one is in college. I don't ever
                   have to think about them. What are they
                   doing? If they are out late, I never even
                   think to check. I never think to ever get ner-
                   vous. Never. Because if they are late, they
                   will be home a little later. They are never
                   up to anything. I don't mean to say they are
                   little saints or anything. They are little
                   stinkers. But I don't have to worry that the
                   cops are going to bring them home in a
                   hammer-lock. I don't have to worry that
                   they are hurting anybody. I am sure that
                   beer and cigarettes enter into it. But I don't
                   worry. I have thought so many times, "How
                   odd it is. How different." I was a nervous
                   wreck whenever I opened my eyes and Tim
                   wasn't right in the room.

Comment on Tim

Tim showed a variety of behavioral problems, including violence, theft, and fire-setting, and his behavior seems to have
become worse after his parents divorced. Tim's father seems to
have favored the other children in the family and to have
belittled Tim. The father also had violent tendencies and mood
swings.

    Tim was in counseling on several occasions, but the
counselors identified few signs of serious disturbance, and they
appear to have been correct. There was little in Tim's childhood

and adolescence to indicate a severe psychiatric disorder, and nothing to indicate that he was potentially suicidal.

Tim gave very few clues to an impending suicide. Notice that initially Tim's mother said that there were no clues at all. But later in the interview she mentions several occasions on which he mentioned suicide or a depressed mood.

From the interview, Tim's mother seems to have been an average woman, caring for seven children after her marriage had broken up. She worked nights, but she managed to find a little time for Tim to help him understand his problems and to help herself cope with him. But it did not work. Her life is easier now that Tim is dead, and one wonders whether she had unconscious desires for Tim's death.

After Tim's suicide, there was grief, a search for reasons for the suicide, and self-blame among both his mother and his brothers and sisters. Tim's mother seems to have helped her children overcome the feeling of blame by saying that, if anyone was to blame, it was her. The friends seem to have rallied around the family, and there was no social isolation or stigma attached to them because Tim committed suicide.

Interestingly, Tim's mother consented to the interview, which I taped and which I show to my classes with her permission, so as to give Tim's life some meaning. Though she had no advice to offer about preventing suicide, she hoped that the interview would sensitize others to the risk of suicide in loved ones so that they might be better able to prevent suicide. This is a common reaction in those who lose a loved one. Mothers whose children have been killed by a drunk driver or by guns have formed groups in recent years to fight the loss of life. The death of an adolescent seems to be such a waste that we are often driven to find a use and thereby a meaning for the life.

REFERENCES

Calhoun, L.G., J.W. Selby and C. Abernathy. 1984. Suicidal death. *Journal of Psychology* 116:255-261.

Calhoun, L.G., J.W. Selby and M. Faulstich. 1982. The aftermath of childhood suicide. *Journal of Community Psychology* 10:250-254.

Calhoun, L.G., J.W. Selby and L.E. Selby. 1982. The psychological aftermath of suicide. *Clinical Psychology Review* 2:409-420.

Calhoun, L.G., J.W. Selby and J. Steelman. 1988-1989. A collation of funeral directors' impressions of suicidal deaths. *Omega* 19:365-373.

Calhoun, L.G., J.W. Selby and P.B. Walton. 1985-1986. Suicidal death of a spouse. *Omega* 16:283-288.

Glick, I.O., R.S. Weiss and M.P. Parkes. 1974. *The First Year of Bereavement.* New York: Wiley.

Goldney, R.D., N.D. Spence and P.F. Moffit. 1987. The aftermath of suicide. *Journal of Community Psychology* 15:141-148.

Lukas, C. and H.M. Seiden. 1987. *Silent Grief.* New York: Scribners.

Range, L.M. and J.W. Kastner. 1988. Community reactions to attempted and completed child suicide. *Journal of Applied Social Psychology* 18:1085-1093.

Rudestam, K.E. 1977. Physical and psychological responses to suicide in the family. *Journal of Consulting and Clinical Psychology* 45:162-170.

Rudestam, K.E. 1990. Survivors of Suicide. In D. Lester, ed., *Current Concepts of Suicide.* Philadelphia: The Charles Press.

Sheskin, A. and S.E. Wallace. 1976. Differing bereavements. *Omega* 7:229-242.